Vagabond Shoes

=

Jean Burnett

Chetwynd Books
Bristol

Published in Great Britain in 2008 by
Chetwynd Books
19 Newport St
Bristol BS3 4ST

Copyright © Jean Burnett 2008

The right of Jean Burnett to be
identified as the Author of the Work
has been asserted by her in accordance
with the Copyright, Designs and Patents
Act 1988.

This book is sold subject to the conditions
That it shall not, by way of trade or
otherwise, be lent, resold, hired out or
otherwise circulated without the publisher's
prior written consent in any form of binding
or cover other than that in which it is
published and without a similar condition
including her condition being imposed upon
the subsequent purchaser.

ISBN 978-1-5300669-9-5

Printed and bound by RPM Print & Design
Chichester

To my children David and Charlotte, fellow travellers

Acknowledgements

My grateful thanks are due to Little Brown and Virago Press for permission to quote from *Love Among the Butterflies* by Margaret Fountaine, to AK Press for permission to quote from *Sister of the Road: The Autobiography of Box Car Bertha* (Dr. Ben Reitman), to the Bolitho family for permission to quote from the journals of Maria Caroline Bolitho, to Summersdale Books for permission to quote from *The Nomad* by Isabelle Eberhardt, to Carly Lee and Kevin Grieves, to Jonathan Harry at RPM, to my fellow members of the small, but perfectly formed Bristol Women Writers' Group for their unfailing support and advice, and to all the people who helped, cheered and enlightened me on my travels.

Every effort has been made to contact other copyright holders.

JB

Contents

Prologue "She is all irregular and always wandering."
1. France - Travels with my Angst and Others 1
2. Cordes - Fred and Ginger meet the Cathars 16
3. Prague Never Lets You Go 28
4. Prague - The Gypsy's Curse 39
5. Hungary/Romania - Many Strange Things 54
6. Georgia - Pomegranates and Kalashnikovs 70
7. India - The Wheel of Life 81
8. India - Desert Days 92
9. Travellers' Notes 101
10. India - Karma 109
11. Daspan - Varanasi 119
12. Interlude 128
13. LA LA Land and Beyond 135
14. San Miguel - Guanajuato - Frogs in the Market 148
15. A Taste for Space 156
16. Oaxaca - Vera Cruz 162
17. Merida - Small Mahogany Men Wielding Machetes 181
18. Cuba - This Isn't A Tale of Derring Do 188
19. Izamal - Tulum - Gods and Devils 202
20. Merida - Taxco - The Honorary Consul 210
21. Puerto Vallarta - Ending on a High C 217
22. California – Home-The Journey is its Own Reward 228

Prologue

This meander around a large slice of the planet was a modest attempt to follow the example of a bolder group of women who, although restricted by corsetry, were free to roam a less troubled world unhindered by passports. Some of them carried guns, although they seldom used them. One woman carried a ceremonial sword and even the most spartan of them took along a folding bath.

My experiences were less dramatic and more modest. I had no entourage or guns, very little luggage and no folding bath. Despite these differences my motives and experiences were surprisingly similar to those of my Victorian forbears.

It has always been difficult for women to be serious voyagers, to get away…to leave everything behind. Constricted by love, domestic responsibilities and lingering gender expectations, running away is seldom an option once a female is past the gap year stage. I was fortunate in being able to step outside my ordinary life in middle age and connect with my inner dromomaniac.

As a child I can recall hearing my adult relatives complaining "she's wandered off again." Like Lady Mary Wortley Montague I was "all irregular and always wandering."

My experiences on these travels were generally good ones. People were kind and helpful everywhere with a few exceptions. As another Victorian traveller noted, if you're a woman they try it on more.

I hope that my good fortune will encourage others to escape for a while. After all, if Victorians in corsets could do it…bon voyage!

Jean Burnett

1
France - Travels with my Angst and Others

The idea had germinated when I first saw my friend's sports car in a field on the Isle of Wight. She was leaving for New Zealand and the car was for sale - a pale blue Fiat Bertone popsy of ancient vintage, in good condition but a little frayed at the edges. This description could also be applied to me so I was sure we were meant for each other.

'It's a boy racer's car' said a bystander.

'I'll have it' I said, quickly handing over some of my meagre capital. I imagined myself careering around the byways of England in an open top car, my hair blowing in the wind like Toad in Kenneth Graham's *Wind in The Willows.*

'It's only held together by will power' the bystander added.

'The pipe work is solid copper,' I replied as I climbed in resisting the urge to exclaim 'Poop! Poop!'

I called her the Blue Bombshell. It was not so much a case of leftover life to kill but a last chance to hurl myself through the Gates of Life before Time's Wingèd Chariot caught up.

On moving day I closed the front door firmly behind me.

'You forgot to take the lawn mower,' my brother reminded me.

'I shan't need a lawn mower,' I pointed out. 'I won't have a house any more, or a lawn.' We walked to the car in silence as the removal van disappeared in the direction of a warehouse in Avonmouth where my goods and chattels would be stored for an indefinite period. I had suffered a life crisis, as it was tactfully described. A new phase had to be entered into, a path re-negotiated at this comparatively late stage.

I had sold my house in the middle of a housing slump and paid off my debts. Any money remaining would not buy a home anywhere I would want to live. The days of juggling a family, a lack-lustre career and a tottering mortgage were over, but one option remained - to run away - a course not often open to middle-aged women. I would take the remaining money and run; see the world before the rocking chair beckoned. A few enduring fantasies could be made flesh, some ambitions realised. Afterwards, who knew? With luck I might never need to come back.

Time seemed to change its shape during that strange rehearsal period for my new life. Within the space of one week I had bought the sports car and attempted to buy a suspiciously cheap apartment in a crumbling Gothic mansion complete with mock-Jacobean banqueting hall and cheap plastic bathrooms in situ.

'It isn't attached to the mains,' said the estate agent nervously, fearing for my sanity. It had been good enough for one of Queen Victoria's ladies-in-waiting who had lived there in the 1870s, and it had been love at first sight as far as I was concerned. I could hear people saying 'I know this weird but wonderful woman who lives in a Gothic ruin.'

Overcome by common sense at last, I abandoned the idea and returned to my parents' house in London. Depressed by being in this situation at such a late stage in my life I considered various options while the universe expanded and contracted hourly without benefit of chemical substances.

I would go to India and offer my services to Vandana Shiva, an eco-heroine of mine. I would go to a writers' retreat and finish my novel - twenty five thousand words on the computer already after only ten years. I would leave everything and cycle around the world. I later dismissed this idea due to a bad back. I didn't think the Fiat would be up to it either.

I would work as a caretaker in a palazzo in Tuscany; eventually marrying its owner, an undemanding millionaire of mature years. I was rapidly losing touch with reality but what had reality ever done for me? During my more desperate moments I even toyed with the idea of becoming a nun. I had heard that religious orders were short of vocations and I wondered if they might have relaxed the rules sufficiently to accommodate a lapsed catholic with a nicotine habit, a cat, the oldest sports car in captivity and a case of deep-rooted cynicism.

Later I made a list of these options and stared at them for a while. Perhaps I would try them all. Definitely I would become a genuine eccentric, a batty woman, one of Germaine Greer's crones. I would be interviewed on Breakfast TV; I would have my fifteen minutes of fame.

I shook myself and went to buy a coach ticket to Paris. I had decided to model myself on that handful of unlikely and extraordinary women travellers in the Victorian era who were always described as "intrepid." Most of them were restless, eccentric and probably insane. I felt a tremendous empathy with them.

One of them was Maude Parrish an American who had run away from an ill-fated marriage in San Francisco at the end of the nineteenth century. She described how she had been around the world sixteen times with her "Nine pounds of luggage and a banjo."

So I ran away. I hurried more than if lions had chased me. Without telling him. Without telling my mother and father. There wasn't any liberty in San Francisco for ordinary women. But I found some. No jobs in offices like there are now. You got married, were an old maid or went to hell. Take your pick.

I had also lived in San Francisco for several years after I

married. Maude and I shared the same ideas about travelling light although I ruled out the banjo. I had a vague idea that I might live cheaply in some obscure corner of the Third World.

Another traveller who started out late in life was Isabella Bird who explored the world on horseback from the Rocky Mountains to Ladakh, from Malaya to Morocco. At first glance I had little in common with Isabella, separated as we were by more than one hundred years and an ocean of conventions, beliefs and restrictions; but closer inspection revealed enough similarities to make her an acceptable role model for my travels.

On the down side we had both suffered from bouts of depression and we both looked to travel, to the freedom of the road to cure our ills, or at least to provide a lengthy escape from them. Isabella had no financial problems and I had many. Only once was she stuck for a little spare cash. In Colorado in November 1873 she confided in a letter home that she was...*feeling the pinch of poverty rather severely... When I have paid my bill here I shall have exactly twenty-six cents left. The Denver banks have suspended payment and would not cash my circular notes.*

Neither of us had been married for more than a few years. She had no children; mine were grown up and independent. Nothing held us back. I doubted that Isabella had ever flirted with the idea of taking the veil. She had never needed to carry her own luggage and therefore had no understanding of the concept of travelling light. At least I did not have to worry about packing silk petticoats and corsets, although her Hawaiian riding habit sounded more attractive than shorts and trainers.

Isabella had travelled everywhere on horseback. At the age of seventy she rode a giant black stallion in the Atlas Mountains of Morocco, mounting from a ladder. Maude Parrish had travelled to the Klondike by steamer and dog sled. My mode of travel would be less romantic.

A friend had advised me not to get too introspective and Freudian about my situation. Freud had been into sex and isolation, she assured me, and was therefore an unreliable guide in the post-feminist era. She suggested that we might travel to India together for an audience with the Dalai Lama.

I left the Blue Bombshell and the cat a few weeks later, full of regret that I couldn't take either of them with me. A journey to South West France by coach, ferry and train can take almost twenty four hours. I could probably have reached the Dalai Lama in much the same time but I had decided to take my stalled life and my unfinished manuscript to a writers' retreat in the Lot and Garonne region. This would be the first stage of my journey around the planet in search of an answer to my problems. I just wished I knew what the question was.

My family had been discouraging about my plans and my children, despite having enjoyed dashing around the world during their own gap year, were curiously reluctant to see their mother doing the same thing. I decided they all had my welfare at heart but I would ignore them and leave, regardless.

I was taking the longest, slowest and cheapest way, but I had all the time in the world - nothing but time in fact - a privilege available to the jobless, the retired and the romantic. Speed is not a consideration for the real traveller. *"The great affair is to move,"* as Robert Louis Stevenson remarked. Time was like a big, fat chocolate cake that I was going to sink my teeth into. That great traveller in Arab lands, Freya Stark, agreed with Stevenson, *"It doesn't matter if you arrive today or tomorrow."* The great travellers of the past experienced a certain level of discomfort as the hallmark of a serious wanderer, a badge of honour, if you like. In view of my tight budget I fully expected to experience that side of things.

The coach was half full with students, an elderly back packer and me. It left Bristol at midday and seemed to take an extended wander around most of South East England before arriving at the channel port. We stopped in odd places like a supermarket car park in Witney. Nothing very much happened, the students disappeared for a while and the elderly backpacker kept to himself. I joined the driver outside for a cold drink and a cigarette. Coach travel often has a surreal quality, well known to the young, the elderly and the poor, the only people who travel this way.

The long haul to Dover gave me the opportunity to see my past life unfurling before me in catastrophic detail. I tried not to be Freudian but I wondered what I was "into." Like most women I wanted money and someone to carry the luggage but both of these items were eluding me. I was into writing, flamenco dancing, Hardy and the Brontës; I was a member of the Dracula Society. I was one of those people Anita Brookner writes about whose lives have been ruined by literature.

I had lived in California, Mexico City - and Watford. More recently I had lived in a backwater whose name, literally translated, meant "The strong man who lives by the creek."

I could count my blessings: I had never been a Playboy bunny, although born at the right time, I had not been christened Concepçion, and I still had all my faculties. Soon I would be old - moi? I once believed that success meant being able to afford three years of Jungian analysis to enable me to find out who I was. Now I knew that I really did not want to know. Anyone who aspires to be a writer needs to nurture their angst, hug their neurosis to their breast. Lose it and a lifetime of writer's block beckons.

By the time I boarded the ferry I had reviewed my entire life, reliving the worst episodes from my embarrassing convent education to the ecstasy and pain of childbirth and divorce, the despair of lost love and the shock of realising that I was only five feet tall. I had always felt six feet.

Exhausted and cramped, I finally tottered onto the ship, which was so full that it was only bearable to stand on deck. I watched the dark mass of the English coastline disappear into the night as a Greek chorus played in my head.

'You can't travel alone, it's dangerous for a woman,' translated as 'a woman of your age.' People whose experience of abroad was restricted to renting a gîte in Brittany for two weeks in August assured me that Central America was a particularly bad area for a lone female. Someone who had been mugged by ten-year-olds in her child's school playground told me that Mexico was a notoriously violent country. She had read about it in the Guardian.

As for Cuba, one of my proposed ports of call, it was probably safe on the streets because it was Communist, but I would get thrown into prison on the thinnest of excuses. India was one place where a companion or two would be useful, but all that was in the future. I inhaled the aroma of night air and frying onions, which instantly said England to me and told myself that I was becoming paranoid.

The Greek chorus had not troubled Maude and Isabella. As soon as she got on to the steamer Maude knew she was among kindred spirits,

Here I saw people I could understand. Here were those in the flesh who had lived and travelled in my mental map of Old Mother Earth. Imagination is a grand and stimulating thing like a cocktail, but to find reality is like a full course dinner with champagne.

Isabella had set off resolutely into unknown territory with her silk underskirts and her distressing, politically incorrect attitude towards ethnic minorities. She wrote of *"Irrepressible niggers"* and her opinion of Native Americans was not high. They were all *"Hideous, filthy, swarming with vermin, savages."*

Pushing my way through the crowds on board I realised that most of us were rapidly becoming filthy and sweaty, if not actually verminous. I went down to the coffee shop and managed to find a seat next to a young, female backpacker. Her body and her pack were patched with dozens of tattoos and badges, her feet safely encased in Doc Martens.

We started to chat and I told her that I was starting a year-long odyssey around the world. She looked doubtfully at my large suitcase and the loafers on my feet but made no comment. We talked about the lure of the open road and I told her that like Lady Jane Franklin, the wife of an Arctic explorer, I had always had "*A bit of a peripatetic turn.*"

Somehow the conversation touched on Robert Louis Stevenson; I told her how much I had enjoyed his *Travels with a Donkey in the Cevennes* when I read it as a child. This provoked a violent reaction: did I not realise that Stevenson had been very cruel to Modestine the donkey? I had failed to notice the Animal Liberation slogans on the backpack. The conversation seemed to flag after that and I went in search of a chair for the rest of the night.

Bodies were sprawled across stairways and someone occupied every seat with two fractious children. I finally settled into a chair designed by a sadist for a dwarf and tried to sleep. I reflected that Stevenson had certainly had a potent effect on my wanderlust. His maxims had stayed with me since I first joined a library at the age of five after lying about my age. The wall had been emblazoned in gold letters with the words *"To travel hopefully is better than to arrive."* I was planning to put that sentiment to the test in the months to come.

In the middle of the night we arrived in Calais and resumed meandering gently in the direction of Paris. Somewhere outside Rouen at lunchtime that day the vehicle broke down and we sat drinking convivially in the garden of a country inn for an hour or two until a replacement arrived.

In Paris I dragged my luggage around the metro to Montparnasse station and boarded the TGV for Bordeaux. I had ignored the advice of Emily Lowe (*Unprotected Females in Norway; 1857*), *"The unprotected should never go beyond one portable carpet bag."*

I had a faint regret that the days of white serge travelling suits and leather Gladstone bags were over mingled with gratitude that I was not obliged to pack a tea kettle and a harp, as one lady traveller from the past had done.

On the train, watching France flash by, I read the words of another Victorian traveller:

'*I left England in the autumn of 1862 intending to try whether the south of France really was a cheaper place of abode than England. I travelled (for a lady) in a rather peculiar fashion, for I took with me only one small waterproof stuff bag, which I could carry in my hand, containing a spare dress, a thin shawl. Two changes of every kind of under clothing, two pairs of shoes, pens, pencils, paper, the inevitable 'Murray' and a prayer book, so that I had no trouble or expense about luggage. My plan was to locate myself by the week, in any town or village that took my fancy and ramble about on foot to botanize, and see all that was worth seeing in the environs; and as I was a lone woman, I took for my companion a mischievous but faithful and affectionate rough Scotch terrier, to be my guard on long solitary walks. I resolved also to mix as much as possible with **the people**.*'

Mary Eyre was obviously a resourceful woman for the time who was bothered very little by either convention or punctuation. I was not sure what a Murray might be but I decided that the Rough Guide was probably a good substitute. I had to forego the faithful Scottie but my laptop would accompany me everywhere on this leg of the trip.

I left the train at Bordeaux and travelled for an hour on a

local line. My host and hostess were waiting on the platform.

'How was the journey?' Monica asked. I shrugged and smiled thinking of my animal liberationist companion.

'We've put you in the cow-byre,' Monica told me; 'you'll be very comfortable.' Remembering the saga of the apartment on the Isle of Wight I replied,

'I'm sure I will, as long as it hasn't got an avocado bathroom!'

On the drive to the house they told me the story of their departure from England, the selling up and the conversion of a barn into the proposed writers' centre. The converted cow byre was a delightful place with an azure blue kitchen and well-stocked bookcases. The only problem was lack of light so I tried to write outdoors when the wind allowed.

My host and I wandered around the complex like lost souls. They lived in the original farmhouse, a small and rather ugly building next to the cow byre. The huge barn conversion, proud and beautiful in its unheated splendour stood on the other side of the pool. Monica and James sank all their money into the project but there were too few customers to make it profitable. Because of this they could not afford to live in the barn themselves.

There was an edge of desperation about the couple which became apparent every evening after dinner when large amounts of the local plonk had been drunk and nightmares, barely suppressed all day, came screaming to the surface. I feared that my own presence did not help as I came with plenty of desperation of my own. Will James ever finish his novel? Will I finish mine? Will Monica get enough clients for her next course - and will I ever get to India?

Outside the complex there was nothing but the rolling fields of prime French farmland with those charming champagne coloured cows dotted about. French farmers, shored up by EC subsidies, roared about in tractors all day and most evenings. Excitement consists of gossiping about the shooting of a neighbouring farmer's dog; was it an accident or a grudge fulfilled? There was very little to do and even fewer people to do it to or with.

James had one luxury, satellite TV and a plentiful supply of BBC videos. Monica's luxury seemed to be the local red, which she bought in large plastic containers. James pondered on the quirks of French life. He asked me if I knew that the French take more tranquillisers and buy less soap than any other nation in Europe. I said it was probably because they invented Existentialism but he had already lost interest in the subject.

'Buenos Aires has more shrinks per person than anywhere else in the world,' I commented.

'What does that have to do with anything?'

My hostess loaned me an ancient bicycle so that I could cycle into the village to buy my baguette and other supplies. I careered along the two mile stretch of road struggling with the stiff pedals and very low handlebars while village dogs tried to bite the tyres and village people gave me curious looks. I discovered that only old ladies in black used this means of travel. Old men rode Mobylettes and wore berets while sensible people drove 2CVs.

I bitterly regretted leaving the Blue Bombshell behind in England but I was too cowardly and absent-minded to drive on the right. It was my own fault for assuming that I could go around the world on local transport. Bus services in this part of the world were as rare as whooping cranes, my sense of isolation was frustrating and I was reminded of women I had met in California who couldn't drive. They spent a lot of time standing on their front porches waving at passing truckers. They also cried a lot.

Travelling around the French countryside was meant to be done in an open-top sports car. Edith Wharton taking a "motor flight" through France in her own splendid vehicle was driven by an obliging husband at the dawn of the automobile age.

A short afternoon's run carried us through dullish country from Chartres to Blois, which we reached at the fortunate hour when sunset burnishes the great curve of the Loire and lays a plum-coloured bloom on the slate roofs overlapping, scale-like, the slope below the castle.

Wharton's travel writing was shot through with a novelist's perception, full of colour, light and shade, as in her description of a visit to Nohant to see the grave of George Sand.

A gate leads from a corner of the grave-yard where George Sand and her children lie under an ancient yew. Feudal, even in burial, they are walled off from the village dead...On the whole, the grave-stones at Nohant are disillusioning, except that of the wretched Solange, with its four tragic words: La mere de Jeanne.

I tore myself away from musing on George Sand to be rescued by a young woman friend of Monica's who was visiting with her two small boys. Vivica was Belgian, recently divorced from an Englishman and living in France. The little family lived outside the village in a very basic rented cottage, miles from any neighbours. While the boys swam in the pool she confided that she wanted a place where they could be alone and peaceful. After an unstable childhood and two divorces she was striving to give her children something she had never had - roots.

Vivica drove me around the area in an elderly Citroen, introducing me to the delights of Quillan, Valence and La France Profonde. We passed turreted manor houses abandoned by their English owners who had bankrupted themselves in their restoration. The British presence was almost as strong here as it had been during the Hundred Years War. The bastide villages, fortified against the English invader, were now being restored by new invaders, affluent retirees, second homers and seekers after the good life. The local French continued to battle against the region's high unemployment levels while their children migrated to the big cities.

We drank in shaded bars or worked her overgrown garden as we discussed various ploys for putting our lives back on track. I, at least, had the option of moving on. France was only the first stop on my route. Vivica planned to work in a Swiss hotel when her sons visited their father.

We trailed around Valence on market days eating lunch specials, buying herbs from the Vietnamese refugees who lived in their own village, and inspecting estate agents' windows. There was also a sizeable North African community in the town that filled the locals with fear and loathing. Vivica laughed with continental glee as I delighted in the glaze on a brioche or the crispness of the lettuce.

'You don't understand how awful English food can be,' I told her.

'Yes I do, I've been to Liverpool!'

Monica and James had plenty of visitors at the house, a mixture of French and English people. The latter had settled in the area and some of them seemed even more desperate than my hosts. One man entertained me with a blow-by-blow account of his battle with the British Government which was refusing to pay his pension. For months he had lived off the good will of friends and the farmers he assisted. He explained that the local cattle were his hobby, especially since his wife and daughter had left him. I raised my eyebrows in alarm but he assured me that he was an expert in bovine fertilisation.

I pondered whether artificially inseminating French cows was freakier than my own passion for novel writing and flamenco dancing on a scale from one to ten.

'He used to own a hotel,' James explained, 'but his ex-wife got the lot.'

Geoff had taken his pension battle to Brussels and with the

aid of the social services section of the EC, staffed entirely by the Irish, Westminster had been defeated. We all applauded this example of Euro-power in action.

The French visitors were more demanding than their English counterparts. The French want to draw you out, make you contribute. It makes for a more exhausting but interesting encounter. An English couple from Bergerac arrived one afternoon with a French-Algerian woman who seized me around the waist and danced with me in a passionate clinch while James' tapes tangoed in the background. Nobody found this at all odd but I had never smooched with a woman and I felt very gauche and embarrassed.

When the visitors were gone the miasma of desperation came down again. Even my hosts' dog was accident-prone and usually sported a bandaged paw.

'The other dogs gang up on him,' Monica sighed.

On my cycling trips to the village I gradually got to know the local characters - the postman who was one of the pied noirs – 'We had thirty servants back in Algiers;' Madame Amaury who was eighty seven and ran the tabac – 'I have never voted since Le Grand Charles passed away.'

I discovered that the large garden centre in the village was owned by a British couple and in a nearby village an Englishman had rescued the failing local bakery. I was curious to know the reactions of local people to this invasion by their traditional enemies, les rosbifs, but the answers I was given were inconclusive. On one hand there was gratitude for anything that helped to revive the moribund French countryside coupled with understandable resentment about foreigners taking over.

Some of the ancient inhabitants of the surrounding villages must have fought in the Resistance during the war. When I saw them eyeing the incomers speculatively I wondered if they were trying to remember where the guns were buried.

2
Cordes - Fred and Ginger Meet the Cathars

Among the many visitors to the retreat were an English couple who lived near Cordes, the ancient walled city further south that I wanted to visit. They promised to arrange a cheap place for me to stay when they returned home.

Eventually, they contacted Monica to say that I could stay with friends of theirs who lived in the oldest part of the town. The woman was from England, a musician who was married to a cello maker of Spanish origin. I later discovered that he was one of the most gifted makers of string instruments working today, with world famous artists among his clients.

Monica said that my living costs would be low but there was one small problem, which she was sure would not bother me. My antennae pricked up at this point. We were sitting in the spring sunshine by the swimming pool drinking the local poison.

She explained that the couple owned a museum of musical instruments in a converted medieval house in Cordes. There was a small, studio apartment at the top of the building where I could stay free of charge in return for occasionally helping out in the museum on open days. Of course, I would be alone in an old, probably haunted building at the top of endless flights of stairs, but she was sure that I would be able to cope with that.

In fact, Monica did not exactly say all of this but it was implied. I was not going to let a little eccentricity prevent me from visiting Cordes and I accepted at once. There was a tiny note of relief in Monica's voice which made me wonder whether I had almost outstayed my welcome at the centre. I knew that several members of their large respective families were due to arrive and they probably needed me out of the cow byre.

I set off a few days later on another train journey deeper into rural France. Monica and James waved a warm goodbye. James looked relieved at not having to carry my suitcase again. I changed trains at Toulouse and travelled on a local line which stopped at the nearest station to the aptly named Cordes-Sur-Ciel.

The town itself is built on top of a mountain and the station is a few miles away on the plain. There is now a small, blue Disney-like train on wheels that takes tourists and faint-hearted locals from the foot of the mountain where the market and most of the shops are situated, up the almost vertical streets into the old town. I decided to take a taxi up to my new hosts' house near the ramparts.

Their home was beautiful; a carefully restored fifteenth century town house full of dark beams and nooks and crannies, with a touch of Laura Ashley chintz furnishings. A régime was worked out so that I could bring my washing to the house and liaise with them about museum opening hours.

My hostess offered me a portable radio suggesting that I might find the silence in the old building a little oppressive. I had a twinge of alarm at this point but I had already burned one set of boats and I felt obliged to live dangerously.

It was almost dark when Toni drove me to the building. The old cobblestones of the square in front of the museum rang like bells as we walked across to the huge oak door criss-crossed with iron bands. There were no lights in any of the neighbouring buildings, which were all either museums, galleries or restaurants that would not open until the summer season began. The sole street lamp sputtered and died as we stood at the door. Toni said that was always happening and she would have to speak to the Mairie about it.

The door eventually opened with a groan and after a little

groping the hall was flooded with light. We trailed up several flights of worn stone steps passing floors of exhibits - instruments, sheet music, pictures and a small shop selling CDs and tapes. It was all beautifully laid out but I scarcely appreciated it at the time. My imagination was working overtime, the silence echoed around us and I had always been afraid of the dark.

'You aren't afraid of the dark, I hope?' said my hostess, not waiting for a reply. She opened the door of the large, bare studio under the eaves, which was sparsely furnished with a bed, a desk, and a couple of chairs. A very large expanse of floor stretched between the door, the bed and the small window. Later, in daylight I would enjoy the wonderful view over the rooftops of the old town but at that moment it was just a porthole into the night. I quickly pulled the curtains across while my hostess deposited some milk and eggs in the neat kitchen. In the morning I would find a bakery nearby where I could buy a baguette.

The kitchen looked well equipped and there was a tiny shower room hidden behind another recess. The radio was plugged in, Toni told me to sleep tight and minutes later I was alone. Terrified that the wan 40-watt light bulb in the studio might die on me I undressed, dived into bed and pulled the covers over my head. Every ghost and vampire story I had ever read surfaced to torture me but I was tired enough after my journey to fall asleep very quickly.

During my time in Cordes I never adjusted to the sepulchral silence and emptiness of the museum at night but I grew to love the place. I had always wanted to live in a Gothic house and at last I had achieved my ambition, if only for a short time.

I grew adept at racing up several wide, stone staircases before the landing lights went off. As I burst through the wooden door at the top and switched on that dim studio light, relief and a feeling of triumph would sweep over me. I would drink luscious French chocolate knowing that I was safe from the hobgoblins lurking below. Occasionally I wondered about previous assistants at the museum. Had they simply moved on or had something more sinister happened to them? I didn't want to raise the subject with my hosts, not wishing to look a gift horse in the mouth.

Nothing would have induced me to open the door after I had drawn the bolts across. If fire had broken out I would have crawled through the window over the crooked rooftops. When I learned more about the blood-soaked history of Cordes and its part in the Cathar wars I wondered uneasily about what had happened in my building at that time. My hosts told me that many of the houses had needed to be exorcised, their thick stone walls still echoing with the screams of the tortured.

Some people think that living in Georgian Bath is like living in a museum but the people of Cordes live in what is essentially a city-sized torture chamber. These chambers may have been converted into chic cafés, impressive museums and houses with a certain twisted charm, but the atmosphere of terror continues to press down with an almost physical weight.

In the late afternoons as the light was beginning to fade in the oldest and emptiest part of the town, I would wander around the narrow, cobbled streets near the ramparts where the panic oozing from the stones seemed almost palpable.

In between the smart, converted apartments other houses awaited the attentions of the developers, their rusting iron-barred doors and eyeless windows gazing into black nothingness. This dismal legacy has done nothing to diminish the town's popularity. Like Bath it is a world heritage site and, like the city of Minerva, its property prices are beyond the reach of all but the very well heeled. I would have moved there instantly if I could.

Cordes, built on its dark mountain is, in bizarre contrast,

surrounded by the beautiful sun-drenched countryside of Languedoc. When I took my washing down to my hosts' house the scent of lavender and herbs mingled enticingly with the eternal French aromas of coffee and chicory and hot bread. I had long chats with Toni and we discovered a mutual fondness for tap dancing and the films of Fred Astaire. She was worried by my nocturnal terrors and offered me several videos to play on the giant TV screen in the museum.

I was too frightened to go downstairs to play them at night, but often in the afternoon I would open the shutters on the third floor so that shafts of sunlight criss-crossed the rows of lutes and violas in their glass cases. Then I would tap away in unison as Fred and Ginger were putting on the Ritz. I wondered what the Cathars would have made of that.

I quickly became accustomed to my museum chores; the locking and unlocking of the massive front door with its wide iron bands was the most difficult task. It may have been original and ancient but the electronic alarm system was definitely hi-tech and the ritual had to be completed each time I went in or out.

Every day I would open the creaking wooden shutters on each floor, grappling with the iron hooks and closing them again during the hottest part of the afternoon.

On museum open days I operated the video which showed the history and process of instrument-making, after I perched in the little entrance hall selling tickets and souvenirs. I had memorised a short speech about the place but I dreaded any complicated questions which would tax my French which was not bad but not brilliant.

The museum was full of quirky, idiosyncratic objects such as the world's smallest violin. Another quirky object was the telephone, which was connected only to my host's house - a nice touch of French economy.

Some of the cafés, galleries and museums were beginning to open for the season, but food shops were not in evidence.

Only the bakery functioned nearby, all other groceries had to be purchased down below at the foot of the mountain in "new" Cordes. This was enjoyable enough; the market was a delight and a small supermarket was packed with everything a gourmet could want, but the journey back up was daunting. I resolved never to take the blue train and I managed to stick to that most of the time.

The older people who had lived there all their lives ran up and down the almost vertical streets like mountain goats. After a few days I found the upward slog more bearable - very good for the heart I told myself. Present day Cordes was certainly a much healthier place than it had been in the past. On my way up I passed a number of doctors' offices and a First Aid post for stricken tourists. The chief torturer's house now sold CDs and postcards and housed the tourist bureau.

I did not get to know many local people because the locals invariably turned out to be foreigners. The bakery was run by a Swedish woman, the little ice cream bar by a South American. The Swedish baker simply preferred life in France and had found a way to finance it.

'They needed a bakery here,' she shrugged, 'so I opened one.' Felipe had escaped from the troubles in Argentina.

'I just wanted a peaceful life,' he told me as I ate yet another of his pistachio specials.

I came across several English expats who had settled in Cordes including an elderly English couple who had an apartment to rent in the old town. Their faces looked familiar and I discovered that he had been a well-known TV actor from my youth and that I must have seen his wife around my old stamping ground in Hampstead. We had probably passed each other in Waitrose on the Finchley Road.

Patrick had a severe heart problem and was bed-ridden. He held court on the sofa in the tiny, oak-beamed living room praising the wonderful French health service, which was entirely free for him. He spoke of being rushed into clinics in nearby Albi whenever he felt unwell; no waiting lists, no problems, deluxe surroundings. We agreed that it would be awful to grow old in the UK without a good deal of money.

The couple had moved to France with their children twenty years before and had lived in various rural spots until they arrived in Cordes. A town on a mountaintop seemed an odd choice for a man with a severe heart condition. Patrick was a prisoner in the house, unable to negotiate the mountain or even the steep steps outside his home. This insouciant approach to the problems of life endeared them to me. It was good to know that I was not alone in frequently making the wrong decision.

As I struggled up and down the streets with my packages I dropped into a succession of art galleries, antique shops and hairdressers, chatting in franglais to the various proprietors. I found that most of them were perfectly happy to remain in Cordes most of the time but Albi was near enough to provide anything extra such as a cinema, a library or a bigger shopping centre. It was not long before I went off to explore Toulouse Lautrec's native city for myself.

I was impressed by the excellent library and over-awed by the huge, rose-red fortified cathedral which looms over the centre in a threatening manner, probably designed to remind recalcitrant Cathars that the Vatican was watching them. The Toulouse Lautrec museum was next door to the cathedral. The atmosphere of Albi was typical of the Midi, relaxed and laid back, but I was told that many young people found it provincial and they longed to get away to the brighter lights of Toulouse or Montpellier.

An Englishwoman who had lived in Africa and had decided to put down roots in Languedoc ran one of the galleries in Cordes. One evening she invited me for a meal in a rural restaurant alongside the bubbling River Cerou. As we enjoyed the food the proprietor and his wife told us that they would soon close down due to lack of customers and high costs. During this depressing conversation he also informed us that the river was highly polluted, although efforts were being made to clean it up. Despite this the area was popular with the English who had bought many of the more picturesque local homes.

I felt a real affinity with the town but I decided it was time to move on. The next horizon was beckoning and I had resolved to spend a year travelling, so travel I must

I took a local bus to France's equivalent of Hay-On-Wye, the book town of Montolieu. The town was really a large village in which almost every shop was a bookshop, with a few restaurants, the requisite tabac and a boulangerie for essentials. I had heard there was a residential café in the village where writers could rent rooms. It sounded perfect.

The writers' rooms above the café were simply furnished with some attractive French Victorian pieces. The bathroom boasted the usual array of copper pipes with a tub big enough for three. Coming down into the café in the morning for a coffee and a croissant was very satisfying. Living in a restaurant must be the ideal existence for a writer, although men might prefer a bar. Freedom from domestic cares together with regular gourmet meals felt like heaven while removing any lingering excuses for not getting on with the novel.

I took to writing at a table outside in the narrow alleyway where mimosa bloomed in small courtyards. My fellow writers were two French women, long resident in the USA, who returned each summer like pilgrims for a breath of French air. Delectable smells wafted in from the café where lunch was being prepared. Lucia would poke her head out into the alley to tell us that there was a vegetable soup on offer followed by a salade Niçoise and cherry clafoutis. After that very little work would get done.

The fourth writer was an American girl who arrived a few days later. She didn't appear to do any writing but she assured me that she was gestating the great American novel of the zeitgeist. The three of us found her rather annoying, brash and too rich. We reproached ourselves for this.

'She's only a kid,' we chorused.

When not in France, Anna "chilled" in an Italian hill town in the Arezzo called Poppi, which she described as idyllic. To have the money and time to divide your life between these delightful spots would be perfect. I favoured living between Hay-on-Wye, Cordes, Poppi and one of the white towns of Andalucia. Hemingway did something similar as he wrote his way from Spain to Cuba to the Florida Keys. A private income or a couple of successful novels would be the first requirement.

I suppose that memories of France are inextricably linked with food and drink. I remember my first trip abroad to Bayeux as a schoolgirl, sent by my school to a Benedictine convent for French improvement, as it was termed. My chief recollection of the town, apart from regular Sunday afternoon trips to admire the Tapestry, was the enticing smell of gingerbread, pain d'épice, on which I spent most of my pocket money. I haven't smelled that heavenly odour for a long time.

M.F.K.Fisher, an American traveller in Dijon in the 1920s, remembered the same treat... *a smell as thick as a flannel curtain.*

As I explored the shadowy, narrow streets of old Bayeux I found strange, unadorned little shops where I was entrusted to buy black head pins for the nuns' veils, Gitanes cigarettes for our assistante and, when money allowed and no teachers were around, more pain d'épice. It was cut from large slabs and wrapped in colourful paper. It's not surprising that I had tooth trouble in later life. Fisher believed that the recipe for pain d'épice had been brought from Asia by a canny crusader.

The café's staff consisted of the two young female

owners, an American and an English girl, and two helpers who were working their way around the world. At the end of the season, on the first of October, the girls shut the doors, packed their bags and set off on travels of their own, returning the following Easter to open up again.

One evening the local poet arrived, a larger than life woman in black silk and baroque jewellery with a small boy in tow. She invited us to her house in a nearby village. Françoise was a native of Audes, France's last and forgotten district.

'It's the end of the world' she assured us, 'that's why I like it.'

By this time I had explored every bookshop in Montolieu and watched several games of boules between the residents and the visitors and a diversion seemed like a good idea.

The poet's house was undergoing renovation and resembled a building site so we sat in the garden where I tried to keep up with the rapid-fire French going on around me. Françoise presented me with a book of her poems, privately printed. As I helped her in the kitchen she told me how she had driven around France for a year with her small son, living in a camper van. She was escaping from an abusive husband and, 'Trying to exorcise my demons.' Now she was happily settled with another partner and had put down roots in Aude. Françoise tried to persuade me to buy a house in the village. She thought we might run some sort of literary B&B. I needed little persuasion to chase another fantasy that involved leaving my problems behind in England.

'Stay here,' she said, 'it's close to England. You don't need to go anywhere else.'

We looked at a suitable house nearby but the local convent owned it and the nuns were driving a hard bargain. Later, Lucia from the restaurant drove me around the villages to look at houses for sale, each one more remote, dilapidated and impractical than the last.

Eventually I dropped the pretence of looking for a house and took a bus to Carcassonne, another fairy tale city that is not what it seems. Purists sneer at Carcassonne, the turreted medieval city that was so enthusiastically restored by Viollet le Duc in the19th century that it is perilously close to Disneyland.

The real Carcassonne is a pleasant southern town with the river flowing at its feet. As I walked across the bridge and up a steep hill in the hot sun the turrets of the walled city gleamed enticingly enough. Close up, the mass of coaches in the car parks and the hordes of tourists pouring through the gates reflected the malaise of the century, too many people peering at too few sights.

Back in Montolieu the whole village seemed to have been invited to an alfresco supper in the ruined mill area down by the river. This large complex was being restored by an English family; a heroic and absurd project that caused the locals to shake their heads over the mad Brits. It was an opportunity to meet the sort of amiable, intelligent weirdos who are likely to congregate in a book town. I had met the same types in Hay-On –Wye. We drank a great deal of the vin ordinaire of Languedoc-Roussillon and made a toast to the new owners as we surveyed the extensive débris of the derelict buildings. Their children played happily among the abandoned, rusting workings in defiance of all health and safety regulations.

I spoke to a couple of young men, an Englishman and an Australian, who had spent time in Prague, which was to be my next port of call. They were able to give me some useful tips about life there, adding helpfully that I could get a coach straight to Prague from the nearest town. 'It just turns up on Thursday mornings.'

A few days later it was time to pack and say goodbye.

The Café du Livre had a fascinating visitors' book filled

with contributions from its literary guests. Poems, short, short stories, witty comments and fanciful recipes made a pleasant change from "very nice" and other malnourished comments usually found in such pages.

I contributed a short murder mystery with apologies to Hercule Poirot called *Murder at the Café du Livre - a Franglais crime passionel.* This was a surreal fable about a mysterious woman, her companion and a dog that lived on bowls of café frappé. The couple always wore dark glasses and harboured an obsession for the café's Wednesday special. I think the story needed more work.

Thank you, Lucia and Poppy; living in a café is even better than living in a museum. Thanks also to Francoise whose poems still wander around in my head.

"S'il vous plait, forgez moi un mot;" my sentiments entirely.

From France I returned to London to prepare for my excursion into Eastern Europe. The itinerary I had chosen for my travels meant that I had to retrace my steps frequently, my trips radiating outwards like the spokes of a wheel.

My decisions about where to go were, as always, determined by literature. Kafka's city beckoned to me.

3
"Prague never lets you go...this little mother has sharp claws"
Kafka

I had not had time to learn any Czech before leaving for Prague. The long, tortuous coach trip would have been an ideal opportunity to prepare myself with a few important phrases. Neither had I brought along any books or tapes so I could only memorise a few words listed in the Rough Guide. Fortunately, another passenger, an English woman going to the wedding of a Czech friend, offered to teach me some basics.

By the time we crossed the German-Czech border I could say, 'Good day, thank you, I do not speak Czech' and 'Where is the toilet?' As I already knew the word for castle - hrad and that Prague was pronounced Praha, I thought I had made a good start. Later, I discovered that the most useful phrase would have been 'I have been overcharged,' especially in relation to taxi drivers.

I was able to try out my new language skills when we stopped at a run-down, greasy spoon restaurant just over the Czech border. Redolent of Soviet-style Intourism, it was staffed by the requisite unfriendly, apathetic couple who offered us a dark brown soup cowering under a layer of grease. There was also a slice of white bread and a sausage of unknown provenance. Judging by the taste we decided that the main ingredient was soapy wood shavings. All these activities stopped me from dwelling on what I had left behind; my father's recent death and the sight of my daughter's face suddenly crumpling as she waved me off at Victoria coach station. Minutes before she had been giving me crisp instructions in the usual daughterly way, but neither of us liked farewells.

The coach stopped in the centre of Prague and I took a taxi to the agency recommended in the Rough Guide as good for cheap accommodation. When the taxi stopped in a large, deserted square at three pm on a Sunday afternoon I realised that I had no Czech money, only travellers' cheques and some Deutsch Marks. This led to an angry exchange with the cab driver who waved his arms and shouted in Czech. I waved and shrugged in English, saying 'Deutsche Marks' a lot. Eventually he grabbed the money and drove off leaving me at the kerb with a large suitcase in what appeared to be a ghost city.

I was relieved to find someone in the agency who spoke English. She arranged for me to stay with a family in one of the city's apartments for what seemed an excessive amount of money. The woman explained that Prague was a very expensive place; she was emphatic about that, implying that nobody had a right to come to her city unless they had bulging wallets.

'We Czechs are not able to travel at all,' she admonished me. 'Under the Communists we couldn't get passports and under capitalism we can't afford to leave.' Throughout my stay I constantly ran into the sullen resentment of the locals, the post-communist disillusionment. Foreigners, especially Americans, had moved in, prices had rocketed and now Pragers could no longer afford to live in their own city. Prague had become the new Paris, I was warned. I asked politely to be able to change some money for a taxi but I was met with shrugs and more paper rustling.

I dragged my case to the designated address passing six branches of McDonald's but no cash dispensers. My accommodation was in a tall building on a busy main road with several unlit stairwells and corridors, something I became used to in the next few weeks. The apartment was spotless but sparse, the occupier and her daughter polite but not friendly. The bed was rock hard. I became accustomed to all these things as time passed and I moved around the city in search of better lodgings, a more convenient location or simply a kinder landlady.

In total, I stayed in four different areas of the city, all in private homes and at various prices. These stopping places ranged from the city centre to a grim, working class suburb, one of the high rise panalaks (apartment blocks) on the edge of the city and a final resting place with a friend in the elegant, if somewhat run-down area of Vinorhady, a kind of Czech Belsize Park.

Vinorhady was also home to the wonderful U Knickhomolo (The Bookworm) bookshop - a complex of art gallery, café and bookshop where I spent a good deal of time. I discovered books published by Twisted Spoon Press exploring the development of Surrealism, a movement that was born in Prague and which embodied the spirit of the city. The elegant café was a good meeting place for expats, transients and locals alike. The food was overpriced and the wine horrible, but the bread and beer were good and a beautiful, wistful eyed young pianist played tunes from the musicals on a white baby grand piano.

Ivana's spacious turn-of-the century apartment had belonged to her parents. She told me it would be impossible for most Pragers to buy such a place today. It was close to the centre and to the metro station with the longest name, Jiriho Zu Podebrad, named after a Czech king. I always enjoyed returning there, especially when I thought about the place in Zizkov I had stayed in and the various beds I had sampled.

I decided that I would make an expedition out of the city on a weekly basis. Rail fares were cheap and the trains usually reliable, if past their prime. One of my trips was to the town of Kutna Hora, famous for its mummies and the vast cathedral of Saint Barbara.

I spent hours wandering around a town which had all the charisma of Slough on a wet Bank Holiday. Although it was a Saturday there were few shops open and fewer cafés, except for a pizzeria in the main square. I collapsed there, tired and hungry after failing to find the mummies which are preserved in the towns extensive mine workings. Later I discovered that I should have taken a bus to the nearby village of Sedlec.

It was impossible not to find the cathedral of Sveti Barbora, the patron saint of miners. It soared above the rooftops, huge, echoing and virtually empty, built by the local miners but never quite completed. In one corner I found a small, exquisite fresco of a unicorn, the ancient symbol of virginity. It seemed totally out of place in this overwhelming and intimidating building with its vertiginous Gothic spires.

Retracing my steps I found the station I had arrived at was now closed. I discovered there was another station somewhere but it was growing dark and I started to worry about getting back to Prague. I took refuge in the Hotel Meridien in the main square, ordered a beer and wondered what to do. While I was pondering on the frustrations of not being able to communicate with anyone, I watched a man at the bar out of the corner of my eye. He didn't move a muscle for half an hour, and then he moved one arm slightly. Czech drunks were either singing at full volume or frozen to their glass.

Eventually I managed to convince the hotel receptionist that I need a taxi, saying 'Station...Praha' to the driver in a pleading voice. He deposited me some way outside the town where the presence of a large crowd on the platform convinced me that I must be in the right place. There were no signs indicating where anything was headed so I followed the crowd onto the first train hoping it wasn't going non-stop to Moscow.

'Praha?' I enquired of everyone.

'Ya! Praha.' they chorused. I wedged myself into a corridor full of young conscripts in ill-fitting uniforms going home to mum for the weekend. The reek of the toilets mingled with the aroma of the ubiquitous Czech sausage being munched by everyone. The journey took forty five minutes and various people tried to communicate with me in sign language, Czech and odd words of German. I smiled and nodded and they laughed hysterically. I had a feeling that the joke was on me.

I spent a few days following my arrival trying to track down the only contact I had in the city; a woman I had corresponded with who worked for the US Peace Corps. Her particular concern was with helping women in business and would-be female entrepreneurs. I had offered to work as a volunteer in the office.

I found that Fran's office had been moved and it took some time to locate the new address. My wanderings around the old centre gave me a chance to orientate myself and I eventually found the place in a run-down building in the same huge square where I had arrived the previous Sunday afternoon.

Fran and her Czech assistant, Elena, became good friends of mine during my stay in the city and through them I found a network of English speaking residents - Czech, American and English. This was important in a place where I couldn't communicate with anyone. I considered going to language classes but eight weeks would not have been long enough to enable me to hold any meaningful conversations.

If I had spent the entire time mute and incommunicado it would still have been worthwhile. Prague itself was the highlight of my visit, the star of the show, beautiful, melancholy, sinister by night and delightful by day. The quality of the rain was different in Prague, the fog more clinging and wispy as it slipped across an age-blackened bridge or settled on the shoulders of a crumbling statue.

According to legend, Princess Libuse founded the city, becoming the country's only female ruler. She chose the spot after seeing a vision of a city whose spires would touch the stars.

The city has a long history of association with the occult which was at its height during the reign of the sixteenth century Hapsburg Emperor Rudolf 11 who kept his court up in Hradcany, the castle complex on the hill, whose spires and palaces dominate the landscape. Rudolf was a mysterious and monstrous figure, obsessed with magic. He consorted with astrologers, magi and charlatans of all kinds, including England's John Dee who was well-known at the court of Elizabeth 1.

High up in the castle square looking down over the red/gold roofs of the city you can feel the strangeness, the impulse to throw yourself down as if into a deep lake. Many observers have commented on this compulsion as they stood in that spot. The crowds of tourists and ice-cream vendors have not lessened the urge.

Prague has always been the dark heart of Europe, the centre of European decadence, desire and deceit. Its inhabitants have a twisted, love-hate relationship with "The old she-devil," borne of centuries of ill treatment by successive waves of conquerors. Life has always been hard for the locals and nothing has changed. The latest conqueror is capitalism which has brought an illusory freedom accompanied by the bondage of economic decline, low wages and soaring costs.

Many successful businesses are now run by in-comers like the American couple who spent their retirement capital on creating the city's first laundromat. It seemed to be doing very well, although few local people could afford to use it.

The instinct of the people here is to keep a low profile, to let things pass over and to hope for better times. This does not make them a particularly open or friendly crowd.

Everything is suffused with the natural Slav melancholy, the brooding atmosphere of Prague itself and what has been described as the funereal malevolence of its architecture.

Some famous past visitors to Prague have believed that they lived there in a former life, so thoroughly bewitched were they by this city on the Vltava. Before long I chose to believe it myself. I was retracing my steps in some way as I pounded the pavements until the bones in my feet hurt and idled on bridges like Libuse waiting for her magic city to appear.

I would spend half of everyday exploring the city before going into the Peace Corps office or meeting someone for lunch at the rendezvous spot on the corner of Nekazanka and Prikopy streets. Later, I was intrigued to see that same corner used as a meeting place in the Hollywood film *Mission Impossible*.

Gazing at the twin black spires of the Tyn church in the Old Town Square that cast a chill over even the sunniest day, it was easy to imagine Kafka wending his way across to a coffee shop thinking of his twisted plots in this mad, gothic city, criss-crossed with the baroque and the surreal.

I am a word child and names exert a great power over me. Far flung journeys have been planned over many years simply on the basis of an exotic street name or for the picture they conjured up in my mind; the Street of the Assassins in Venice, The Street of the Necromancers in Prague, naturally, – even the Massacre of Glencoe Tea Rooms in Scotland. I have never seen the Street called Straight in Damascus, but it resounds in my head.

On a more practical plane I soon realised that much of the peculiar atmosphere of Prague, its blackened buildings and soupy atmosphere, was due to pollution. Most people heat their homes by burning brown coal during the hard Czech winters. Ancient boilers chugged away all over the city heating the apartment blocks and public buildings and giving off the smoke and fumes that were poisoning the place. The city lies in a bowl and in addition there was industrial pollution of various kinds - a legacy from the Communist era. Noxious Ladas and Trabant cars still filled the streets among the Mercedes of the nouveau riche.

Respiratory diseases were rife during the long winter months and anxious parents tried to send their children into the country from time to time so that they could breathe cleaner air. Young women who have spent their whole life in the city can find their fertility affected.

Prague is still a she-devil, a wicked mother, entrancing her children and killing them at the same time. For distraction they have the best beer in the world, cheap cigarettes to speed their extinction and the novelty of American junk food and Ikea stores which they crave, although they can seldom afford them.

It took some time to understand the peculiar customs and idiosyncrasies of the city. Why was the beer so good and the wine so awful? Why did they not recognise this and concentrate on producing beer? There were other mysteries such as the appalling taste of Czech cornflakes (metallic) and Wenceslas Square, which was not a square but a rectangle, or more accurately, a short, wide street. I often passed the wonderful old Hotel Europa on the Square, a beautiful art nouveau building and the only place to stay in the city if money was not a problem. I was sure that the beds in the Europa were soft and I vowed that I would stay there on my next visit.

Transportation was one of the delights of living in the city. The Russians installed a metro system before they departed - possibly their only benign legacy. It was small but highly efficient and spotlessly clean. On the streets were the ever-present trams, wonderful old Skoda clangers that went everywhere for a flat fare of 40 Kroner at that time. Any car that tangled with these civilian tanks would lose the battle.

One hot day outside the main department store a small Trabant with the registration plates of Lithuania or Latvia had a head on collision with a tram and was squashed into a concertina shape, its two young male occupants meeting a horrible death. Onlookers licked ice-cream cones as firemen removed the victims who were probably on their first post-Communist trip abroad.

On Sundays I would try to get out of the city on trips to places like Karlstejn Castle, thirty eight kilometres from Prague. Once, I arrived at Smichov station to find hordes of mushroom pickers emerging after an early morning foray into the forests. Rubber booted and well wrapped up they carried overflowing baskets of fungi. As I waited to buy a ticket a female backpacker stood in front of me, her rucksack topped incongruously with a child's lilac plastic potty.

The forty minute journey into the countryside was a pleasure, despite the morose company. The carriage was filled with mainly middle-aged people who were not of the generation that willingly engaged strangers in conversation. At Karlstejn I followed the small crowd out of the station along the wooded banks of the Berounka River into the narrow village street that leads up the hill to the magnificent Gothic castle.

The main street was lined with souvenir shops and small cafés, still delightfully chaotic and adhoc. No doubt all that will change in the near future. As the castle gates came into view a trio of costumed trumpeters appeared on the battlements and sounded a welcoming fanfare. Even at Windsor they don't go that far.

I joined a tour of the castle's rooms but the outside is far more impressive than the rather bare interior. The Emperor Charles 1V built Karlstejn as a treasure house and a retreat from the capital. The crown jewels were stored in the Holy Rood chapel, but the jewels are now elsewhere and the chapel was closed to the public. It was possible to see the royal apartment where the reclusive Charles refused to see anyone, including his wife, who eventually smuggled herself into the castle disguised as a man.

Looking out over the peaceful green valley it seemed like excellent walking country and I wished that I could have stayed awhile before returning to relentlessly urban Prague. Whenever I felt this way I would walk up to Petrin Hill or to the royal garden at the Hrad to glimpse some greenery in peace and quiet.

From a particular corner of the Royal Garden there was a bizarre corner view of the mad contours of St Vitus' Cathedral, enhanced on one occasion by an unusual art exhibition. In a pavilion nearby I found a dozen or more alabaster skulls carefully lined up on the floor. It could have been something decreed by the crazy Emperor Rudolf himself.

I had admitted to Fran that I worked in journalism and PR and she persuaded me to give a lecture to the Business and Professional Women's Association. The day was approaching and I was having a major attack of nerves. I wanted to practice my speech aloud but it was impossible in my lodgings; the owner would have been alarmed. Practising in public would be even more eccentric.

In between times I continued exploring the city finding places like Hybernska Street and discovering that the Irish connection had been a congregation of Irish Franciscans in the Middle Ages. Today, the Irish presence in Prague is through theme pubs, which are breeding throughout the world. I once came across an Irish pub in a small Italian village.

By this time I knew all the important tram routes although I never mastered the bus system. The metro was a pleasure to use as I discovered when I developed a bad cold and a hacking cough that refused to clear up. Elena insisted I should go to her husband's clinic at the end of a metro line.

He and his colleagues were paid abysmally low salaries but the hospital was clean and modern and I was seen immediately – no NHS problems here.

I was examined and given a prescription for medicine to be collected from the pharmacy next door. There was no fee. As I left, I tiptoed across the shining tiles in the entrance hall which an attendant was carefully buffing with her felt overshoes.

Over dinner with Fran and some friends one evening I declared that it was time to leave my lodgings. I needed to find somewhere cheaper. The others looked doubtful and said that I would have to move some distance from the centre of town. Everyone had a horror story to tell about accommodation. Fran herself was into her third year in a cramped apartment in one of the high rise buildings known as panalaks that fringed the city. These had been built to house the workers during the Communist years. At least Fran's flat was subsidised by the Association and also included a washing machine - a rare luxury for most Pragers. I decided that I would have to return to the unwelcoming lady in the accommodation agency.

4
Prague - The Gypsy's Curse

I duly gave my lecture to Fran's business club for women and it was well received. The concept of public relations and media relations was a difficult one for people to grasp when they have grown up under a Communist system. The idea of a free press was in itself a revolutionary idea usually greeted with derisive laughter rather than acceptance. Getting across to my audience that the world would not come to them to buy their goods and services was the first task. Many of the business women in the audience seemed appalled at the amount of time they would have to spend selling their products and services in a variety of ways. The idea of intense competition seemed unbelievable to them. I felt like a teacher trying to convince a classroom of teenagers that trigonometry was relevant to their lives.

I quickly explained the principle of writing a press release and then asked everyone to spend ten minutes writing a short piece about their own business. Despite their misgivings they quickly adapted to the idea and produced some excellent promotional pieces.

The problem of actually dealing with the press was another matter. I had seen for myself that in this very macho society businesswomen were not taken seriously. When a male journalist was invited to one of the club's meetings he tended to write about the length of the women's skirts rather than the businesses they ran.

Afterwards, Fran said she thought the lecture had gone well. The women, together with the rest of Czech society had to make a fifty-year leap in a very short time. Their attitudes and the general development of society were set in a 1950s time warp; the Women's Movement had passed them by.

When Fran had started the club the members could not understand why they shouldn't bring their husbands. The concept of a women only anything seemed unthinkable to them.

Now that foreign influence is so strong in Prague and advertising agencies are opening up, business people will find it easier to make the leap forward. Female entrepreneurs were not lacking in dynamism. I met some formidable women in Prague but they all accepted their second class position without question. Their energies were also dissipated in ways that are fortunately unknown to us. Could their fellow club members be trusted? Had they been members of the Communist party before the velvet revolution...were they informers? I found that the returnees were equally mistrusted. These were the Czechs who had managed to flee the country in the past and were now returning in large numbers. One member who was particularly helpful to me had spent several years in Canada and now found herself an outsider, resented for her Western knowledge and for taking the easy option, as they saw it.

I was introduced to more Czechs and a few more US Peace Corps members, most of them located in obscure parts of the Republic and in Slovakia. The organisation has lost much of its gloss since the glory days of the Kennedy administration. Workers complained that they were the forgotten people, disregarded at home and often paid late. When they returned to the US after their three year stint they found job hunting difficult. Employers tended to regard a period in the Corps as an extended holiday.

Nobody could offer any advice about moving my lodgings so I returned to the agency again. My pleas for cheaper accommodation were met with an incredulous stare. The receptionist leafed through her file and produced a card which she held at arm's length with evident distaste.

'Try this place in Zizkov,' she said in a tone which implied that wild horses would not have dragged her there.

'What is Zizkov like?' I asked innocently. Her face became blank.

'You can get there on a tram,' she muttered, avoiding my eye. It did not sound promising but I had little choice. On the tram I read the guide book which described Zizkov as a run-down, working class suburb favoured by gypsies and low-lifes. I noticed that the tram seemed full of care-worn women clutching large bags of laundry. As we travelled farther from the centre the area became featureless and dismal, full of public offices and Soviet-style avenues.

When I eventually reached the street address I found it was a place of tall, grime-blackened Victorian tenements. I dragged my luggage up several more unlit staircases to another small room with a very hard bed. The beds were growing progressively harder. How did they do it, I wondered? I imagined a factory somewhere producing these rock-like bed sandwiches and probably winning a special Soviet award for its efforts.

My new landlady was elderly, very religious, and obviously neurotic. She spoke no English and clutched a large crucifix as she followed me around the grim apartment. The bathroom was the most antiquated I had ever seen, probably untouched since its installation at the turn of the century. The landlady herself occupied one room where she also slept. The TV was permanently on and she sat surrounded by drying washing.

Each morning a continental breakfast would be set out for me, its price written neatly on tags attached to the cup. The income from unwary tourists like myself was probably all that kept her from destitution.

Tucked into my penitential bed for the night I read the autobiography of George Sand, a woman of spirit who dragged her lover, Chopin, and two children to Majorca in winter in search of somewhere warmer and different. The island proved to be an unwise choice. Finding that she couldn't buy or rent any furniture for their meagre accommodation, she wrote,

I suppose the only way to repair the folly of coming here is to leave straightaway.

I knew I would not survive long in Zizkov: I was seldom worried about returning there at night despite the deserted, unlit streets, but the depressing atmosphere was beginning to affect me. If I moved immediately I might find myself somewhere even worse. Poor George and her consumptive lover had that problem on Majorca.

An acquaintance, doubtless with the best of intentions, did us the ill turn of finding us a country house to rent. It was the villa of a wealthy burgher who consented to rent it to us for a price modest by French standards though rather steep by those of the island. It was furnished like all Majorcan homes with camp beds, beds of wood painted green and beds composed of two saw-horses on which a couple of boards and a thin mattress had been laid; the inevitable straw-bottomed chairs; tables of rough wood; and, as a crowning luxury, glazed windows in almost every room.

Apart from all of that, everything was fine. I knew just how she felt, although she had the consolation of a beautiful view while I could see only the façade of the tenement across the street.

Then I had the good fortune to meet Paula when I was buying a train ticket at one of the stations. I saw a plump woman with blonde hair awry waving her business card at arriving tourists and I stopped to speak to her. Paula was a jolly, middle-aged woman who rented out half her apartment to visitors. She lived in one of the panalaks and she arrived in her car to rescue me from Prague's underbelly saying that I was not the first person who had fled the Zizkov apartment.

The small inconvenience of having to take the metro into the centre was off-set by my new surroundings. The panalaks were a revelation, the Czech equivalent of a high-rise block on a council estate. They were completely free of graffiti and vandalism and other unlovable aspects of Western culture. Warm, clean and cared for, they were surrounded by grassy spaces and located close to the countryside. The lifts always worked.

Paula and her husband were cheerful and welcoming. She spoke fluent, if fractured English and as soon as we met I knew that she was a fellow dromomaniac. All the money she made from renting rooms was spent on travel to various parts of Europe and to see her son in Canada. Her husband remained contentedly at home.

I was introduced to the other guests; two social workers from Hong Kong who spent hours in the tiny kitchen cooking huge piles of noodles. It was an ideal lodging but for the cramped conditions - five people in an apartment designed for two. Paula kept up a flow of funny stories as she served coffee and cream cakes at all hours, mainly to the social workers who refused to leave the flat if it was raining.

One African tourist had stayed with them who assumed that sharing the apartment also meant sharing Paula's favours.

'I had to explain that landladies did not automatically sleep with their guests!' she giggled. I told her that after Eastern Europe I was heading for India and her eyes lit up with longing. I knew she would have grabbed a toothbrush and left without a backward glance - a true addict.

After settling in I continued my wanderings around the old city, crashing out in the English language café/bookstores whenever I felt the need for a salad or relief from cultural overload.

The heart of historic Prague is the Old Town Square with the slender black spires of the Tyn church in the background. The Church of Our Lady Before Tyn is an example of a Gothic structure which has been given a Baroque façade and trimmings; this happened frequently in the 17th century. It is this Gothic/Baroque fusion which gives old Prague its unique appearance. It looks as if a gaunt, black-clad, medieval monk has been given a makeover by Christian Lacroix. The extravagances of both architectural forms must have exhausted generations of craftsmen. Up in the castle complex St Vitus' Cathedral, begun in the thirteenth century, was still under construction in 1929.

Today, the vast square is always awash with tourists crowding into the pavement cafés and posing in front of the Old Town Hall with its intricate astronomical clock.

A new Kafka museum has opened on one side of the square and on the other side the broad Parisian-style boulevard called Pariszka runs into the ghetto, one of the oldest and most mysterious areas of the city, officially called Josefov.

The ghetto was once home to the largest and oldest-established Jewish community in Europe. The strangely named Old/New synagogue was thought to pre-date most of the churches in the city. Up to the late nineteenth century it was a teeming, crumbling, densely packed area, unsanitary and dangerous and so notorious that the authorities decided to tear it down. This drastic attempt at slum clearance left only the most famous synagogues and the Jewish town hall which boasts a clock that runs backwards. The only other celebrated landmark left untouched was the ghetto cemetery; a tiny atmospheric plot where tottering tombstones piled against each other bear witness to a place where one hundred thousand people were buried in layers. Even the trees seemed to weep in this place as if the earth resented its burden.

By the time the ghetto was rebuilt most wealthy and middle class Jews had moved out to more salubrious areas, leaving only the poor, the disreputable and the fanatically orthodox. Witnesses said that the area resounded at night with the cries and shouts from drinking dens and bordellos and the chanting from the synagogues.

The end of this ancient community came when the Nazis marched in during the Second World War and sent the Jews to Terezin (Theresienstadt) where thousands died or were sent on to Auchswitz and Treblinka, their final destinations.

Most of Prague's Jews these days seem to be American, often the children and grandchildren of the ghetto's survivors, lured back to the sinister city of their ancestors. Legend has it that this area by the Vltava River was one of the first stops for the displaced Hebrews after the fall of Jerusalem.

On the Jewish New Year, Rosh Hashanah, Fran and I were invited to the service at the old Spanish synagogue across Pariszka, which was being restored. It had been used as a warehouse under the Communists but it had once been the most ornate and exotic of the city's synagogues. The rabbi had been imported from Chicago and the congregation was mainly American with a few other foreigners.

Present day Pragers get a lot of tourist mileage out of the ghetto which has been designated a State Jewish Museum. The irony is that the Nazis intended to turn the area into "An exotic museum of an extinct people" after completing their extermination programme - and this is exactly what has happened. Throngs of tourists, mainly German, shuffle through the beautiful, starkly simple places of worship that resounded with the ancient chants for centuries and are now entirely silent. The walls of one empty place of worship were covered with the names of victims of the Holocaust.

The ghetto was very much part of magic Prague, enhancing the city's reputation for occultism and weird practices of all kinds. This was especially true during the lifetime of the celebrated Rabbi Loewe who was credited with the creation of the golem.

Legends about the golem abound in Jewish folk lore. It was said to be a huge, shambling, android figure made out of clay that the rabbi created through cabbalistic rituals to be his servant.

Rabbi Loewe's reputation as a philosopher and alleged occultist was so great that the mad Emperor Rudolph 11 sought a meeting with him in 1592, an unheard of event. What was discussed at that meeting was never discovered. Did Rudolph ask for the secret of making a golem? In fact, the legend grew up almost two hundred years after Rabbi Loewe's death. His tomb is in a prominent place in the old cemetery.

The golem stands as a symbol of the troubled ghetto and its community. It is said to reappear on the streets of Prague every thirty three years and I was intrigued to discover that a visitation was due during my stay. Its residence was supposed to be a windowless attic room - which at the current prices would have cost about four hundred kroner per night.

If the golem was a creature without a soul he would probably pass unnoticed these days. His great height and shambling gait would merely cause him to be mistaken for a Northern European tourist. I think I might have seen him on a number twenty four tram.

He could have been the genial, grizzled drunk farting loudly on the metro. Tourists muttered complaints and a small Vietnamese family cowered away from him. Or he might have been among the crowd of skinheads with swastika earrings and wispy moustaches glowering at passers by on the Charles Bridge.

The golem legend goes hand in hand with other myths centred on Prague. The Wandering Jew, Ahasuerus, is said to appear on the streets from time to time and Janacek's opera *The Makropoulos Case wa*s set in the city. It was the story of the singer Elena Marty who had been kept alive for over three hundred years by a magical elixir. Rudolph would have given half his empire for that.

Another favourite walk of mine was around the Mala Strana, the Little Quarter; an area beloved by Czech writers and composers, by aristocrats who built palaces on Petrin Hill and by anyone who is a Bohemian by birth or inclination.

As I wandered along Nerudova Street I stopped to visit the Church of Our Lady of the Victories, the shrine of the Infant Jesus of Prague. This figure is revered throughout the Catholic world but I found it much less impressive than the build up given by the nuns at my old convent school had led me to expect.

The church was another schizoid affair with a severe Lutheran façade. Inside, the Jesuits had created a shrine to kitsch. The holy child stood in the midst of the gilded interior dressed in gold satin and lace. Banks of yellow iris, gypsophilia and sea shells lay at his feet. Tourists milled around buying tacky reproductions of the statue.

Walking around the crooked alleyways and hidden gardens of the Little Quarter it was easy to imagine oneself back in the time of Kafka or Meyrink and a dozen other famous visitors to this place; a time when the city's Gothic heart was more apparent… a time when Prague was not awash with American back-packers asking the way to a cheap hostel, when there was not a single branch of MacDonald's, the old ghetto still stood and intellectuals gathered in coffee houses. The bones of the Little Quarter are still poking through its baroque dressing and those bones are pure Goth.

When I was tired from my wanderings I would rest in a gilded coffee house and eat a cream pastry called rakviçka which means "granny's little coffin."

The other oasis in the city which always beckoned to me was the café bookshop called the Globe. It was situated in a fairly nondescript area of the city, but nearby was the square called Strossmeyerova Namesti, a name that reminded me of

Dr Strosselmeyer in the Nutcracker ballet. There was an impressive, twin-spired gingerbread-style church on one side of the square.

The Globe was run by Americans and colonised by backpackers and Peace Corps workers. The salads were excellent and the notice boards were always full of offers of lifts to other parts of Europe and various backpacker necessities.

Victorian travellers, in contrast, relied on a kind of bush telegraph set up by officials of the British Empire. The Empire's tentacles stretched so far, its influence was so pervasive that one could travel the world with just a letter of introduction, always sure of assistance from a colonial officer somewhere. The female travellers of that period made full use of these facilities. Despite the physical discomforts involved the actual process of getting from A to B was simplicity itself compared with the present day.

The few women who travelled outside the Empire's reach were truly alone such as the Frenchwoman, Alexandra David-Néel, who "Longed to go beyond the garden gate." She travelled in disguise in Tibet where no Western woman had ever penetrated – and very few men.

By this time I was within a few days of ending my stay in Prague and I had been looking forward to showing the city to a friend. During my time there nothing terrible or even moderately bad had happened to me; as soon as a visitor arrived things started to go wrong.

My friend Jan arrived for a few days holiday after ten o'clock on a Saturday night. I trekked out to the airport by bus and metro on a dark, chilly October evening. We finally arrived at the lodgings I had arranged for her around midnight. By the time she had been settled into a typical time warp Prague apartment full of musty Victorian furniture with matching plumbing, I was left to walk back to Ivana's apartment in the early hours. I skirted the local park with trepidation, but only a few drunks passed by singing happily and ignoring me as I scuttled along.

My friend's exceptional height tended to make her a target while I was always able to blend into the background. When we met to cross the Charles Bridge en route to Prague Castle I knew something was bound to happen. I saw her coming towards me, strung about with cameras and multi-zipped shoulder bags. She towered over everyone and had tourist written all over her.

I murmured something about lots of bag snatchers being at work in Prague. She brushed this aside saying that nothing had happened to me. I decided not to say that I didn't carry tourist clutter and I wasn't six feet tall.

As we approached the bridge the tourist crowds were so thick I told Jan to go on ahead so that I could navigate by her. Afterwards I felt guilty about this. I tried to shout information about the statues on the bridge but it was impossible - people were starting to stare at me. It seemed to take hours to get near the castle and we eventually collapsed in a cafe before tackling the cobbled streets on the downward journey.

Once again she went ahead of me, wandering along, her gaze fixed at least eighteen inches above everyone else's sight line. By the time I realised that a number of small children were darting about on the bridge, it was too late. Jan cried out and I saw that her bag was unzipped and her wallet and credit cards were gone. A passer-by nodded knowingly. 'They were gypsy children, the best pick-pockets in the business.' It was only three o'clock but I had a sudden yearning for a stiff drink.

The next few hours seemed very long and were spent mainly in my least favourite venue, the central post office on Jindrisska. Complicated calls were made to England and credit cards were cancelled. Fortunately Jan's passport was in the apartment so that nightmare was averted. She had some money in her suitcase and she seemed remarkably cheerful about the whole thing. I pointed out the route nearby that Kafka had taken each morning to his job in an insurance office. This information was interesting but the stiff drink was more satisfying.

As she was only staying for a few days she was determined to see as much as possible. Undeterred by the previous day's events we boarded the number 21 tram up to the castle, avoiding the walk across the bridge and up the hill. I had made this journey many times by myself; in fact, it was my favourite trip. The number 21 went on past the castle up to a beautiful old monastery and eventually out to a place called Bila Hora, White Mountain, the site of a famous battle in Czech history where the Catholics had defeated the Protestants - a sort of Battle of the Boyne in reverse.

This time things would be different. We were barely half way up to the castle when a gaggle of gypsies boarded the tram, an extended family of parents, children ranging from seven to teenage plus assorted aunts and uncles. They edged rapidly up to the back of the tram where we were sitting. Some of them surrounded a tall, Canadian tourist toting a camcorder; others made a beeline for us. The Czechs on board stared carefully ahead or read their papers. The driver appeared to be deaf and blind.

I rapidly considered the options. I knew that gypsies were often armed with knives but I was not going to surrender my few remaining crowns without a struggle. The gipsies did not seem to be worried about the size of either the Canadian or my companion. After all, they were four to one. The Canadian was using the camcorder as a shield, holding it in front of his face and trying to fend off the hands that were feeling in his pockets and pulling at the machine. Jan was trying to edge to the front door as the father of the group pursued her. I was marooned near the middle door with mum and junior and several others around me. I noticed an elderly gypsy sitting nearby; probably this was grandpa directing operations by telepathy.

As a bus stop approached I made a lunge for the door shouting, 'Thief!' in Czech as the seven year old tried to grab my bag. I shoved him hard and prayed for the door to open. The boy's mother raised her clenched fists, her face twisted in fury. As I leapt off I saw her face at the window yelling a curse at me. Jan gave a scream as she jumped off-apparently she had been goosed by the gipsy who pursued her.

I was just glad that I still had my money; Jan didn't have any to lose. I was a little worried about the gypsy's curse but I figured that I had probably had my quota of bad luck for the decade already.

The following day, undeterred, we decided to visit Mozart's Villa Bertramka. We took the tram to the Andel stop before realising that we were in the Smichov district, home to a large Romany population. As we walked along nondescript streets passed grim tenements we were watched by a large number of dark eyed children and their unfriendly elders. We hurried into the museum wondering whether the news about our adventures on the tram had got around and we were marked women.

Inside the sanctuary of the Villa we wandered in the elegant and curiously bare rooms where only a few souvenirs of the composer remained on view. The house had belonged to some Czech friends of the composer and he stayed there whenever he came to Prague

Later, I showed Jan the beautiful green and white Stavovske theatre where Don Giovanni was premiered. No one can deny that the often sad and taciturn Pragers are great music lovers. It was heartening to remember that after Mozart's lonely death in Vienna thousand of people turned out for his memorial service in the magnificent baroque church of St Nicholas in Prague when the composer's own requiem was played.

I also had fond memories of the opera house as an entertainment venue where it was possible to buy a balcony ticket for the equivalent of fifty pence. Usually, you shared this bargain with crowds of well-dressed German tourists. Life sized statues of the great composers were jauntily perched on the roof of the theatre. The locals tell the story of how, under the Nazi occupation, orders were given to remove Mendelssohn because he was Jewish. As the statue was reluctantly lowered news came of the assassination of Heydrich, the Nazi commander in Prague. Amid the chaos Mendelssohn was quietly returned to his spot.

That evening, Jan and I ate a last meal in one of the many new restaurants serving international dishes. Czech food is tasty and filling if well cooked, but a change is always welcome. We found an Italian restaurant where the food was excellent and the staff entirely Czech. An example of Euro-Fusion, we decided.

By this time the curse of the Rom had begun to take effect. On the following day Jan came to see me off at the bus station. She would fly home a few hours later while I coached slowly across Europe. As we struggled on the metro with my luggage another attempt was made to grab my purse. A tall, Czech youth pressed up against me in the crowded train and the one thing on his mind had nothing to do with a gratuitous squeeze. I hung on to my purse grimly trying to manoeuvre my feet so that I could kick him. Once again, I was successful as we tumbled off at our stop. It was a bad ending to my Prague trip, but I told myself it could have happened on the Northern line in London, despite the fact that it never had during my lifetime. The coach stopped once again at the greasy spoon café near the border and then it was over- I was back in sanitised Western Europe.

As the coach trundled across France I thought about my times in Prague and the attachment I felt to that city of light and darkness. I remembered Kampa Island, a secluded hideaway reached down some steps by the river near the Charles Bridge. It was a small park full of melancholy drooping trees and yellow street lamps piercing the autumn mist, a favourite place for trysts, romantic ones and the more sinister kind. There were one or two cafés occupying the buildings that were once Prague's main laundries. They were small and served good Czech food, especially the one with the whimsically unpronounceable name of Velikoprovorsky Mlymn.

    I scribbled in my notebooks, trying to get it all down while the memories were fresh.

5
Hungary - Romania
"There will be to you many strange things"
Dracula (Bram Stoker)

I was keen to go back to Eastern Europe after my visit to Prague. The lure of the unfamiliar was a strong one – or at least, the lure of the less homogenised half of the continent. An opportunity came when a member of a literary society I belonged to mentioned casually that she knew a man who operated a coach service from London to Budapest. She said the fare was very reasonable and that, in addition, Imre would arrange accommodation for us in private homes. By this time Eastern Europe had got under my skin and I immediately agreed to go.

Six of us assembled one summer Saturday morning under the Westway flyover to wait for the coach. I felt my first twinge of foreboding when the elderly vehicle arrived and I met Imre, the co-driver, director and leader of the expedition. There were some passengers aboard already, mostly elderly Hungarian exiles resident in Britain, visiting home with their UK passports. The director's neurotic wife was also on board nagging her husband and anyone else within earshot.

We hung around the coach as the traffic thundered overhead. There was an unexpected complication due to the non-arrival of the sixth member of our group, who held the communal ticket. Imre had issued the ticket this way to save on his administration costs. He assured us that it would be perfectly acceptable, like travelling on a family passport. Someone went off to make phone calls in an attempt to track down the missing person.

Suddenly, a taxi screeched to a halt beside us; someone rushed to open the door whereupon a small, ancient female fell out and lay in a crumpled heap on the pavement. Imre and the co-driver bent over her and pronounced her dead. He seemed remarkably unfazed by the whole thing saying that the excitement of returning to her homeland must have brought on a heart attack.

The cab driver was throwing up on the sidelines and a frisson of horror rippled through the group but our leader merely stuffed the old lady back into the cab and went to call for an ambulance. By the time we had been visited by police and ambulance crews and had been questioned and catalogued by the authorities, the day was wearing on.

We had an impromptu picnic under the arches, although the events of the day had strangely reduced our appetite for corned beef sandwiches and warm lemonade. Excusing ourselves on the grounds that we had not known the deceased lady we raised our paper cups to her departed shade.

Then it was finally decided that we could leave. The missing ticket holder had still not turned up but we established that she had missed a train and would catch up with us in Belgium. This meant making a detour via Ostend and Zeebrugge. Her mood was not exactly cheerful when she came on board but at least we now had a ticket.

As we drove across Europe on miles of autoroutes and autobahns the Hungarians picnicked on pungent sausage and onions at seven am and the six Brits disgraced themselves by drinking wine and lager in the small hours and becoming tired and emotional.

Austria passed by rapidly with fleeting glimpses of excessively tidy houses and gardens. We drove through Vienna without stopping, passing the gates of the Schonnebrun palace with its fountains playing in the sun. Some of us had forgotten to equip themselves with any change in various currencies as we stopped in motorway cafes in Belgium, Austria and Germany. Forlorn groups passed around a single cup of coffee or soup in the small hours, anticipating the arrival of the Euro.

Things seemed to go smoothly enough until we reached the German border. At the other frontiers we had been waved through in friendly EC fashion without any passport checks. We sat in the coach for an interminable time while an official examined all our travel documents minutely. He implied that our vehicle was not roadworthy. We had suspected this but it was depressing to have our fears confirmed.
He sneered at our group ticket;

'It is not permitted to enter Germany on such a ticket' he pronounced. There was general consternation and anti-German remarks were made sotto voce, but Imre, as always, managed to smooth things over and we were finally allowed to leave.

Soon we were in sight of the Hungarian border crossing and there was a noticeable heightening of tension in the coach as the elderly Hungarians wondered whether their British papers would be respected. This was just weeks before the fall of Communism. However, I was the person fated to provide the final piece of drama.

Young army conscripts toting their rifles came on board as we stopped at the border post. They seemed friendly enough, if a little ill at ease, and we all offered them cigarettes and sweets on the advice of the Hungarian travellers. When they inspected my passport and visa they burst into excited conversation translated for me by the other passengers. Apparently my visa was not in order - it lacked a photograph.

Everyone began to hyperventilate, especially the elderly folk. My friends watched from the windows aghast as I was led away to the cabin at the border post. I was a little concerned but not too worried. I still had two hundred American cigarettes and a bottle of whisky in my luggage, bought for just such an emergency.

When I was escorted inside I was invited to have my picture taken in a convenient booth and asked to pay the equivalent of fifty pence. Everyone seemed to think it was a great joke. The young soldier walked me back to the coach and I gave him a packet of Kent cigarettes. Imre gave a sigh of relief and we bowled down the road towards Budapest.

Our first impression of the city was of the thunder of heavy traffic and the high level of pollution. We had a home stay arranged in one of the outer suburbs of Pest, the sprawling modern part of the city. Historic Buda on its hill lay on the other side of the Danube.

Our host was an elderly man with a spacious house reminiscent of the ones I had known in Prague; unmodernised, it could have featured in one of those black and white English films of the 1940s and 50s. We had difficulty finding our way back to the place because we could not pronounce the name of the street, but the water was always hot in the shower and our host brought us a bowl of cherries as a welcome gift. We had no languages in common so communication was difficult. Eventually, he decided that we were Yugoslavs and we didn't argue.

Buda, when we arrived there, was a beautiful area with carefully preserved palaces and churches and good facilities for visitors. Most tourists were Americans looking for their roots. I attended a mass in the cathedral that had once witnessed the coronation of Hungary's kings. A small orchestra accompanied a magnificent choir throughout the service.

I had been warned that the Danube was no longer blue, but it did not deter us from taking a trip by boat that gave a good view of the vast, overpowering Parliament buildings and other monuments lining the shore. These lowering buildings, Gothic in style, dated from the days of the Austro-Hungarian Empire.

Local people relaxed on Margaret Island as we cruised by

over the brown, Windsor-soup-coloured water. I was pleased to discover that one can take a trip along the Danube from Budapest to Vienna, or vice versa, on a hovercraft for a reasonable price. I imagined skimming along this waterway, over the burden of so much European history with a Viennese waltz playing in the background.

The highlight of our wanderings in Buda was a visit to the wax museum; a satisfyingly surreal experience tinged with the gothic for good measure. The mini-Tussauds had an atmospheric wine cavern in the basement; a carefully mocked up tourist trap, now de rigeur in Eastern Europe. The exhibition was devoted entirely to the life and works of Attila the Hun, the country's greatest hero.

We trailed behind our English speaking guide, listening politely as he eulogised the man described as the Wrath of God. A looming shadow could be made out as we rounded a corner in the dimly lit rooms. We admired a panorama of the Mongolian steppe as an immensely tall Norwegian towered over the little guide contradicting his hymns of praise in deadpan English.

Guide, (reverently), 'He was a very great man.'
Norwegian-'He was a bloodthirsty barbarian.' After a few exchanges of this nature the guide was visibly quivering with rage.
Norwegian-'He murdered his own son.'
Guide- 'It was a mistake...anyone can make a mistake!' As a last throw he sputtered, 'He was good to his mother.' As we sniggered helplessly in the background the Norwegian said seriously,' how can you possibly know that?'

After the Norwegian wandered off we tried to make amends for our mirth by inviting the guide for a glass of Bull's Blood in the cavern. He almost wept into his sanguine drink as we offered condolences, willing ourselves not to crease up.

After we gained a grip on ourselves someone remarked,
'Foreigners have no sense of humour.'

'No, that's not true,' said another, 'they just have more national pride than the English. If a foreigner insulted Nelson we would just laugh and agree with him. It's called the cultural cringe.'

We argued amicably about this as we resumed our wandering around Buda, agreeing only that Norwegians tended to be very tall. Our final stop before lunch was in the huge square where equestrian statues of Hungarian kings and chiefs stood in alarming numbers. Pointing at Attila I asked,

'Do you think he really looked like that?'

'How can we possibly know?' someone replied in a mock Norwegian accent.

Workaday Pest on the opposite bank has its own charms. The Café Gerbeaud should not be missed. Famously the gathering place for the capital's writers, intellectuals and Bohemians in pre-Communist times, it still glittered in Viennese Empire opulence with chandeliers, ornate décor and a great deal of gilding. The elderly, robotic waiters also appeared to be frozen in time. Someone suggested they might be holograms.

The impressions I had formed of Hungary and its capital in my youth had been largely gained from the plots of Viennese operettas. I didn't agree with Rosita Forbes' impressions, recorded in 1928 when she was a journalist for the Daily Telegraph.

I shall always like Hungary. It reminds me of England. That is an illogical reason, for I have generally been happiest out of England. But the Puzta plain reminds me a little of Lincolnshire, which is part of my blood and bones. I love riding endlessly across the monotonous flatness, not at all lush, with small faint flowers among the grass, flocks of geese, brown sheep and shepherds in their white woollen cloaks and leggings. The Puzta is Biblical in its unchanging simplicity. I like to visualize it under the rush of Magyar horsemen which once saved Christian Europe from the war lords of Tartary.

Hungary did not remind me of England but I agreed with her impressions of the capital and the wine.

Budapest is romance exactly as depicted in sugar sweet comedy. The importance of the day is not recognised until it becomes night. Then the cafés blossom along the streets...we drank the most delicious Tokay. It reminded me of apricots on an old brick wall.

Rosita, despite her privileged background, was an accurate and sensitive recorder of the countries she explored. In the first volume of her autobiography she ranged from Mecca to La Paz via Eastern Europe, always putting her finger on the pulse of the societies she met. Her impression of the rabid anti-Semitism and loathing of the gypsies in Hungary is as true today, despite the fact that few Jews remain in that area and the Romany people flee the country whenever they can.

On the only occasion when I went for a walk alone in the local park I was accosted by a middle aged man who spoke English virtually without an accent. Desperate to speak to a foreigner he told me that he had spent years in a mental institution because he was a dissident. I knew that this was a favourite method of silencing people in the Communist era. In the course of the conversation he mentioned that he had lost many family members in the Second World War.

'We were on the wrong side,' he shrugged and smiled. 'We backed the wrong horse, isn't that what you say?' This led to a conversation about the Holocaust. Looking at me very seriously he remarked, 'The Germans were wrong to kill the Jews because they are a clever people, but there was no problem about disposing of the gypsies because they are just ignorant thieves.' I thought about this remark for a long time after. I am not often left speechless but I was on that occasion.

Getting around the city continued to be difficult; few

people spoke English although German was widely understood and we relied on one of the group for interpretation. I managed to learn "Ambassad Angol" to direct cab drivers to the café in the square next to the British Embassy. This place became our rendezvous spot where we sat watching the huge numbers of gypsies plying their various trades.

Apart from the ubiquitous violinists there were a number of women in their colourful long skirts and head scarves begging, with babies clutched to their breasts. This became known in the group as the dead baby scam. We were convinced that the babies were either dolls or ominously still.

Occasionally we would strike lucky with a taxi driver who turned out to have worked in England for a few years in order to save up for his Mercedes. One helpful fellow gave us his vivid recollections of life in Ealing. It was impossible to use public transport because the impenetrable Hungarian language consisted mainly of consonants.

Meals in restaurants were always fun due to the gypsy music and general gaiety but I found the food a little too heavy for my taste. Our first meal consisted of plentiful fried carp and spiced Hortobagy pancakes, delicious on that occasion, but on a daily basis gulyas and sour cream, pancakes and fried foods plus the liberal use of lard can be too much. I preferred to stock up with a supply of high quality paprika which was so good that I couldn't bear to use it when I reached home. It stayed carefully wrapped in its little case in my kitchen.

The return journey in Imre's coach was a repeat of the outgoing one, mercifully without the corpse or the lost ticket, but featuring several breakdowns.

'Fancy a trip to Istanbul?' was his parting shot.

I fulfilled my ambition to stand in a Transylvanian graveyard at midnight and to look down on the Borgo Pass at a time when the Ceausescus were still in power and their demonic influence could be felt in every corner of that strange country. At the time, Maramures, the most remote area of Transylvania, on the Russian border, was out of bounds to foreigners.

Something can usually be arranged in these circumstances and with the assistance of some well-disposed officials a group of Bram Stoker enthusiasts gathered at Heathrow and prepared to board an elderly Tarom jet apparently held together by string and willpower.

The airpcraft's interior was stark and comfortless with hard seats and grim-faced stewardesses. No refreshments of any kind were served but we had been forewarned and produced our own picnics. The crew looked on in disgust at this evidence of Western decadence. Later I spotted a Romanian passenger furtively nibbling some black bread and sausage when the crew were busy elsewhere.

Bucharest was eerily quiet when we left the airport. Although it was early evening and still light, a curfew seemed to be in operation. The wide boulevards were empty except for an occasional tram or official car. We were staying at the Plaza Athenée hotel, a grand, peeling mansion whose heyday must have been circa 1903. Inside it was dreary and run-down with dim, flickering lights and a mysterious absence of water, hot or cold. The tub in my room was large and welcoming but the taps produced nothing. A daily game involved running around the corridors to see which room had water and pleading with the occupants to allow us to use it. We also became familiar with the problem of the national grid that made electric light a luxury for a few hours each day.

Only party officials seemed to stay at the hotel, plus a few foreigners, mainly Russian. On our first evening we sampled a hotel meal, chicken paprika with slices of polenta. Most of us found the food tolerable and the wine excellent, but this did not really matter. We had not come for luxury hotels and gourmet food.

Next morning we boarded our blue Iranian-built coach and met George, our driver, nanny and general fixer. He claimed to be Armenian by birth but his ability to charm officials and obtain the unobtainable convinced us that he must be the President's cousin, at least. A young man called Vlad was our official guide. They both bowed theatrically, then George leapt into the driver's seat and we sped out of the capital bound for Transylvania, the land beyond the forest. The country's assorted vampires and werewolves slept on unsuspecting as we began our assault on their lair.

Following the mountain passes we eventually arrived in the lonely fastnesses of the high Carpathians. Small towns and villages would end abruptly and the wilderness would take over. Bears and wolves abound in this area.

'No-one knows why there are still so many in this part of Europe,' said Vlad. I took it as evidence that Romania really is the devil's own country.

In the closed area of Maramures we stood on the river bank looking across at the guards on the Russian side. Vlad became very uneasy and tried to lure us away with seductive promises.

'Look! You can see the Borgo Pass from here......there is a Tuica still in the next village.' Tuica was the Romanian equivalent of poteen or moonshine whisky, brewed from who knows what, colourless and lethal. Back home in England I once managed to light a barbecue with the stuff. In the villages the locals would ply us liberally with it, possibly to confuse us so that we could not tell our Western masters their deadly secrets. These same villagers tied red woollen bows on their horses to ward off the evil eye. Judging from their wretched lives it did not seem to be working.

On a freezing, clear afternoon, heavily padded, we went up into the mountains, passing a broken ski lift. Vlad made a fire and we sat companionably singing songs and drinking plum brandy. A local shepherd toiled up the mountain to greet us accompanied by his dog which wore a barbed wire collar. English animal lovers berated him for this but the shepherd shrugged saying that the collar protected the animal from attacks by wild animals.

Then he got to the point of his visit. He had noticed Julia, our tall, blonde secretary, and had been instantly smitten. Through the interpreter he offered fifty sheep and his hand in marriage. The shepherd was toothless, looked all of seventy and had probably not bathed since 1978. He had an illicit Tuica still, he said, to clinch the deal.

Julia was trying so hard not to laugh that her body shook. The shepherd immediately threw a greasy sheepskin around her and tried to lead her off to his hovel in the hills. By the time we had fully dissuaded him it was colder than ever and growing dark. It was time to prepare for our midnight visit to a Transylvanian graveyard. I remembered the old warning; be careful what you wish for, it might come true.

Julia, now known as the Bartered Bride of the Borgo, declared that she would inspect us all before we left to check that we were equipped with silver crucifixes, garlic and blackthorn twigs. I was not sure what blackthorn looked like and it was certainly too dark to search for any in the woods. I was also worried about my godmother's rosary that I had brought along. I had an uneasy feeling that the crucifix might not be silver at all. I quailed at the thought of encountering the Undead armed only with base metal.

When we assembled in the quiet village cemetery the clock was striking ten, not quite the witching hour but dark as Hades in a village and a country where electric light was generally unavailable. Local homes showed only flickering oil lamps in their windows. A farmer leading his horse and cart spotted our candles bobbing about but displayed little interest. I found that strange, knowing that most Romanian peasants would not dream of standing where we were after dark.

Nothing happened that night and we eventually trailed back through the blacked out village to the hotel which shimmered before us powered by its own generator. On the roof of the building a red light rotated signalling to passing vampires, tourists and peasants alike. At that time we were the only tourists for miles around.

The dark recesses of the Borgo pass were briefly outlined by the hellish glow as we went inside to be plied with a cocktail called Dracula's Elixir, blood red and lethal to foreign stomachs. As I wandered along the corridors of this newly built hotel pieces of plaster fell off the walls and skirting boards quietly collapsed. Perhaps the place was a mirage conjured up by a satanic tourist board for our benefit. Standards were not high in the Romanian construction business which did not bode well for all those monumental palaces commissioned by the Ceausescus. Ancient churches and monuments had been razed to make way for these new monstrosities. Soon every town in the country would resemble Slough on a bad day.

There was a place that has escaped this fate so far. Sigishoara, birthplace of the historical Dracula, Vlad the Impaler, was a lovingly preserved time capsule encircled by its fifteenth century walls, full of cobbled streets and medieval clock towers. Our guide showed us around various churches, Protestant, Catholic and Orthodox, carefully explaining the doctrinal differences. Catholic churches were big and imposing on the "God is watching you" principle while Orthodox churches were small, intimate and colourful bringing heaven closer to earth. Protestant churches generally appeared to be empty.

We visited the house that had been Vlad Dracula's birthplace. A plaque recorded this event. The house was being used as a restaurant and the conviviality seemed at odds with the memory of that fearsome creature who impaled his enemies on wooden stakes, watching their agonies as he enjoyed his supper. An even more surreal note in those surroundings was the discovery of a delicious golden wine called Cotnari which was love at first sip. The proprietor nodded approval of our enthusiasm.

'It is a wine for lovers,' he announced poetically, 'always drink it with someone special.' The wine was deliciously smooth, soft and fruity. I thought of Rosita Forbes and her Tokay like apricots on a summer wall.

Despite his personality defects Vlad remains a hero in his country, credited with ridding the state of the Turkish invaders. His head appears on stamps and his statue is found in many places. Only in recent years have the Romanians become aware of the fictional Count Dracula created by Bram Stoker. Slowly they have begun to create Dracula Tours catering for the interests of tourists who have little knowledge of the historical version.

We pondered on this as we strolled past the ancient walls painted Venetian red and gentian blue. Mosaic-tiled cupolas gleamed above wooden balconies and mechanical clocks, archways showed glimpses of courtyard gardens full of red roses and golden vines. Skinny cats watched over tubs of green tomatoes and scarlet geraniums.

As an antidote we were taken to visit the desolate town of Baia Mare full of concrete block houses and empty squares where children paraded wearing their red Communist Youth neck ties.

In pursuit of Bram Stoker's characters we found the site of the Golden Boar Inn in Bistritza where Jonathan Harker stayed on his way to the Count's castle. The inn has disappeared and in the courtyard where Jonathan's carriage waited people looked down from the balconies of squalid apartments.

In the rain soaked streets of the town the only person who

seemed to be happy in his work was the coffin maker. He had left his stock on the pavement and retired for a siesta. Bistritza's gloom was like the depression that afflicts a pretty woman when she realises she is past her prime. The picturesque houses were in desperate need of a coat of paint while cracked yet elegant shutters swung sadly in the breeze.

'Of course, it could be early closing day,' remarked one of our party. One small shop was open selling cosmetics and haberdashery. I bought a pot of cream for the equivalent of fifty pence that the shopkeeper claimed was the fount of youth. It was royal jelly; I thought I heard the Count laughing in the background.

Several castles in Romania were labelled as Dracula's; many of them were used by him, but not all. Bran castle was much more the Romanian Windsor with Queen Marie's French boudoir on view just as she left it. Her heart was buried in the surrounding woods, but unfortunately its location was forgotten during the Second World War.

What a fascinating and colourful place this area must have been in the 1930s. A whole Central European world has disappeared since that era. Queen Marie of Romania, granddaughter of Queen Victoria, was the Princess Diana of her day. The appetite for news of her life, her fashions and her scandals was insatiable. Rosita Forbes, naturally, was invited to tea with her.

We sat on a couch covered with leopard skins and embroideries, in that Hollywood-esque castle, which suited but did not at all overpower the Queen, beside a tea table laden with agreeable things to eat and Marie-the beautiful, warm-hearted, preposterous woman who delighted in being a queen-forgot all about it. She had the most wonderful hands I have ever seen. The knuckles did not project at all. The fingers were long and ivory-coloured. The shape of them showed strength. She wore an enormous sapphire and two pearls. Her dress was like a medieval abbess's robe, black and close fitting with a long train. When she caught my hand and drew me impetuously after her into another sitting room furnished as an oratory and then into her bedroom, I had difficulty in not falling over her skirt.

When I stood in Marie's boudoir I recalled her beautiful hands and her love of the colour orange. Her name immediately conjured up a pair of hands without knuckles like a Renaissance Madonna.

The citadel of Poenari was definitely Vlad the Impaler's lair. It loomed above a gorge with a river rushing beneath. From these battlements Vlad's wife threw herself to her death when she heard that her husband was coming home from the wars. The latest film version told a different story but the home life of the Draculas was rather different from that of Queen Victoria.

We climbed the fourteen hundred steps to the castle ruins on a hot autumn morning. Imprints of bear claws were clearly etched in the stones and near the top a magnificent green and gold toad sat sunning himself. Could this be Dracula's familiar? Nobody had the courage to kiss the creature. As we made our way down we came across a young soldier doing his national service guarding this lonely monument. He looked half asleep in the sun, clutching his rifle to his chest. He saluted us as we left him cigarettes and sweets. At the bottom we met a group of children who offered us freshly picked walnuts.

'Gom?' they asked hopefully, 'chicklat?'

Amid the brutal modernity of Ceausescu-land we found many reminders of a bygone Romania, a once prosperous and elegant place full of Victorian railway stations and wayside shrines. We saw the cool beauty of Snagov Lake and its monastery island where Vlad the Impaler's tomb was kept neat with flowers and candles. When archaeologists opened the tomb in modern times it was empty. Bram Stoker would not have been surprised.

In the countryside people tended their fields and made conical haystacks, others carved fearful devil masks to keep evil at bay; intricately carved wooden churches were hidden in quiet valleys.

A woman employed by the tourist office showed us a typical Romanian house, its walls covered in folkloric patterns, its beds piled high with embroidered linen. Few Romanians live that way today. Overwhelmed by our flashing cameras and Western opulence she exclaimed,

'You should live for a hundred years!'

Gypsies walked the streets in the towns looking as picturesque as ever, with their horses and mules, their wives and children. When one of our group tried to photograph them they chased him waving axes. We stopped in small, dishevelled cafés, little more than pit stops, which sold thick Turkish coffee to revive passers by.

The copper pots were buried in sand to keep them warm just as they were when Vlad the Impaler's army came this way. The Count was right about this mysterious part of Europe. There had been for us many strange things.

6
Georgia- Pomegranates and Kalashnikovs

After my trip into Eastern Europe I decided to continue heading east and on into the Caucasus. I had a long standing connection with the small Caucasian republic of Georgia. Bristol, where I lived, was twinned with its capital Tbilisi and I had been involved with the twinning committee. As always, my romantic idea of the country had come from literature and dance. Lermontov's *Hero of the Caucasus* was the catalyst combined with visits from the amazing Georgian State Dance Company. I remembered the male dancers who could perform standing on the tips of their leather boots and the women with their waist length dark plaits who had perfected a movement in which they seemed to glide across the stage.

Getting to Tbilisi, Georgia's capital was not easy. British Airways had discontinued direct flights and after mulling over websites I opted for Austrian Airways. This involved changing planes in Vienna where I just had time to race through the airport to catch my connection. I was convinced that my luggage would not join me and I was right. Some things were easier for Victorian travellers.

At Tbilisi airport I joined a long line of people who were being carefully ignored by the few people I assumed were immigration officials. I noted the lack of planes and the grass growing on the runway as an American female diplomat growled,

'It takes as long as it takes. There's still a big hangover from the Soviet era.'

At last I was checked through, minus my luggage, and I spotted Tina, my interpreter, waiting for me. She was wearing a bright red jacket and waving a red rose.

Outside the airport she introduced me to a friend who would drive us into the city.

This fascinating, largely unknown little country was falling apart as you watched. Once part of the Soviet Union, its economy was now in ruins. Alex, our driver, formerly middle class and prosperous, was reduced to driving the occasional tourist around in his battered Lada.

Tourists were not much in evidence, I noticed, as I peered over his shoulder through the car's cracked windscreen. We were screeching along a potholed boulevard in the capital while oncoming vehicles drove straight towards us. The first driver to swerve aside was a chicken.

'It's the Georgian way,' explained Tina. 'We are all anarchists at heart.'

In her apartment Tina laid out a feast she had prepared. Her mother and several neighbours came in to inspect me. All kinds of exotic, unknown dishes were offered; heavenly pomegranate and plum sauces, confections of walnuts, coriander and vegetables and khachapuri - a kind of Georgian pizza.

Lacking a change of clothes in the sweltering city and unable to get any Georgian money I tried to concentrate on replying to the neighbours' toasts in a fairly sober and intelligent manner.

'Look how tired she is! Give her more vodka' they said, as my head fell forward into the aubergine salad.

Tina's apartment was on David the Builder Street in the city centre, named for Georgia's greatest king who liberated the country from the Turks in the 12th century and literally rebuilt the place. The steep, winding streets of the old town were full of graceful buildings with oriental rugs hanging from disintegrating wooden balconies. Tbilisi has been destroyed twenty seven times in its history, either by enemies or earthquakes. Each time it was rebuilt by its determined rulers. Today it crumbles away quietly in the sun, its peeling façades and conical-roofed churches overlooking dusty, unmade roads. A recent earthquake inflicted more damage.

The sensation of hanging by a thread, geologically, politically and economically, was what gave life in the capital an edge. Hailing a taxi, attempting to cross the street or buying a melon in the market were major hazards for everyone and virtually impossible for tourists without help. Tina shadowed me everywhere: few people speak English and I managed to learn only "gamarjobat" an all-purpose Georgian greeting.

On the following day, after waiting for the banks to open, we went to eat in a local restaurant. The man sitting at the adjoining table gallantly offered me the use of his mobile phone to call home. I had forgotten my own and the land lines in Georgia always suffered from acute indigestion.

'Is it true that the English put garlic in their shoes to keep their feet warm in winter?' Zurab, the phone man, was interested in all things foreign.

'Don't be a fool!' growled Alex, our Russian driver. He was a former member of the Soviet athletics team and had often visited the West.

You could see Eastern influences everywhere in this country which lies at the crossroads between East and West. There were several splendid, Turkish-style baths where we wallowed in the sulphurous water amid tiled, oriental splendour. Later we viewed the treasures of the State Museum, peering through the gloom of one of the many power cuts with an apologetic guide who spoke fluent French. Upstairs we tagged along with some American tourists led by a tiny, fiery pensioner who barked, 'Don't move!' at a man who tried to sidestep her lecture.

Mtshketa, the old capital, was forty minutes away from Tbilisi at a place where two rivers converged. Now a world heritage site, Georgia's oldest and most important cathedral was there, Svetiskhoveli, reminiscent of the fortified churches of South West France. Inside it was gloomy and filled with ancient icons, their gold and jewelled surfaces lit only by wispy candlelight. Faded frescoes and weathered stone testified to this ancient Christian culture. St Nino brought Christianity here around 300AD and became the country's patron saint, along with St George. The distinctive Georgian cross was derived from two curved vine stems bound together with the saint's hair which she used to illustrate her message.

Outside the church a man was singing an unaccompanied folk song, a harsh, mesmeric sound. This type of a capella singing dates back to ancient times and once heard it is unforgettable. At a nearby stall selling tapes and religious souvenirs someone started to play reggae at full blast. Undeterred, the man went on singing to the distant hills where Georgian legends say the Virgin Mary is buried in a mountain-top church called Jvari.

In Tandzia, south of the capital, groups of transplanted mountain people lived on small holdings in self-contained villages. The background hills were gentler than the lofty Caucasian peaks of their home province, but avalanches and a lack of facilities had forced them to relocate.

Cows, pigs, goats and the occasional buffalo wandered by as old women plucked us off the rocky road and took us home for tea - a mid-afternoon feast of cherry compôte, tea and coffee, home-made wine, khachapuri and anything else available. By this time I was learning to brace myself for the almost suicidal Georgian hospitality. Any excuses about not being hungry, just eaten, on a diet, my doctor forbids etc, were waved away with the traditional motto "A guest comes from God" followed by the command "Eat!"

Our hostess's son showed us his half wolf hunting dogs then walked with us in the forest down to a rushing river, offering to catch a salamander for me.

'Last year an English cyclist came by,' he remarked. 'We

got him drunk and he slept for twenty four hours. Foreigners don't come by often.'

Lack of time prevented a visit to the wine-growing area of khakheti and the famous cave monastery of David Garedja in the desert country bordering Azerbaijan. Although Georgia is tiny - about the size of Wales, it is amazingly varied with Mediterranean and sub-tropical areas as well as semi-desert and the towering Caucasus mountain range. Getting around was difficult and frequently dangerous. Roads were poorly maintained and there were problems with bandits and guerilla fighters from the breakaway provinces. All of this simply added to the sense of adventure and with an excellent interpreter, a trusted driver and an ancient Lada, we came to no harm.

Tina and I left the hot, dusty capital for some R and R by the Black Sea. Tbilisi to Batumi takes eight hours on a slow train. The toilet facilities were best avoided. At each stop food sellers and hawkers came on board with desperate Abkhazian refugees offering to rent a room to us for two lari per night (less than a dollar).

Batumi has always been the country's seaside resort. Horse drawn carriages were for hire on the tree-shaded promenades, the horses' heads adorned with red ribbons "for beauty."

We ate freshly cooked fish with salad, shashlik and French fries in the open air cafés. Tina swam in the sea while I watched from my deck chair. I had been warned that the Black Sea was highly polluted and this was an oil port, after all.

The city is the capital of the semi-autonomous province of Adjaria, governed by Aslan Abashidze at that time, a warlord from an old ruling family in the region. Approved of by Moscow and the West, he appeared be a popular leader although ordinary citizens seldom expressed their true opinions to outsiders. Life seemed marginally better in Batumi compared with the plight of the average Georgian.

Adjaria's economy has flourished due to the monopoly it claims on border tolls with Turkey. Mercedes rolled by in the spacious streets down town but the side streets were pot-holed and filled with crumbling apartment buildings.

I discovered an amazing oriental-style tea house in the centre, full of carved arabesques and mosaics that might have graced the Alhambra. The women working there beckoned me inside.

'Come in, come in! We don't get many tourists from the West. We'll make Turkish coffee and khachapuri for you.'

'Tell me about your life here,' I said.

'Don't ask!'

From Batumi we began a journey up into the high Caucasus Mountains to the forbidden province of Svaneti, an ill-advised trip according to the Embassy. Georgian friends said we might be kidnapped or shot.

'Svanetians dislike outsiders.'

Tina told me not to worry; she had plenty of friends there and useful contacts.

'There won't be any problem as long as you don't mind about the toilet facilities.' I knew this meant a hole in the ground at the end of the garden. We had already experienced this on several occasions.

We liaised with the province's chief of police in the city of Kutaisi's bustling market, joining a small group travelling by marshrutka (collective taxi). As well as the chief there were assorted locals including some formidable older women dressed in deepest black, their skirts reaching to their ankles, gold teeth flashing in the sunlight.

After a ten hour drive up into the mountains through high passes overlooking turquoise lakes it was growing dark and we were invited to spend the night in a small village with the family of the most formidable-looking of the old ladies. It was another two hours on to the mountain capital of Mestia over even worse roads.

I opened my mouth to make a suggestion, a polite refusal even, when Tina whispered hastily,

'Don't upset them or they'll kill us!'

'I thought you said everything would be all right?' I moaned quietly. 'You said you knew them all.' Tina shrugged in a meaningful way; 'I do know them but they are strange people!'

At that moment I couldn't help recalling a Victorian lady traveller, Louise Jebb, who rode into a wild mountain village near Babylon to be greeted by dancing, screaming, stamping men –

'X,' I said to myself, 'you are mad and I, poor sane fool, can only remember that I once did crochet work in drawing rooms.'

We entered an all-female household, except for a small grandson. These were pretty much the norm in Svaneti where vendettas were still carried on with enthusiasm and the graveyards were full of men who died in their thirties and forties. The custom of bride stealing was also alive and well. One of the old ladies had lost her son who was shot defending the honour of his fourteen year old daughter from a local admirer.

'If they come back again we'll be ready for them,' said granny, grim-faced. She signalled to the boy who went to retrieve the family's prize possession. In the living room he waved the Kalashnikov rifle above his head, shouting a few Caucasian war cries. The old ladies applauded and boasted of their deadly aim before urging me to drink more home-made vodka. This was urged on us at every meal, especially breakfast.

'It's the elixir of life!' said granny number one, her face splitting into a huge grin.

Perhaps because of the vodka I slept well on an ancient feather bed shared with Tina. Before falling asleep I thought ruefully that this would probably be the closest I would come to "untrodden pathways" on my wanderings. Very few visitors come to this area but it is hardly off the map. I had not trekked along the Skeleton Coast of Namibia or across the High Andes. I would need more time, money and resolution for that. Personally, I would not want to be responsible for describing a hidden gem that enticed a horde of tourists.

Rose Macaulay did exactly that, if unwittingly, when she described her car trip around Spain in 1948. In *Fabled Shore* her lyrical descriptions of the area we know as the Costa Brava signalled the beginning of the package tour industry and the concreting over of that once lovely spot.

Spain has changed so much in the last few decades. Could this remote area of Europe eventually share the same fate? When an American traveller, Kate Field, visited Spain in 1875 her impressions of the country were very similar to my own in Georgia. *Spain acquaints one with strange bedfellows*...she was referring to the plentiful supply of fleas. Her encounters with bureaucrats mirrored my own in communist and post communist countries.

I was an American whose stay in Spain was limited to a few days. Could I have my trunk?
'No.'
'Why not?'
'Because there is cholera in Paris.'
'But I haven't come from Paris'....

O tempora! O mores! I fell asleep dreaming of Spain and woke to find my cheeks wet with tears.

When we finally arrived in Mestia we found a very small town surrounded by the distinctive Svan towers-fortifications built in the Middle Ages and still used today. The main square was desolate with burned out buildings, a legacy from the civil war in the early 1990s and incursions by Abkhazian fighters. There was no longer a hotel or even a café.

'We are the forgotten people of Europe,' said the guide at

the local museum as she showed us dusty, priceless books and ancient icons lying on open shelves. 'Only God protects these treasures,' she added sadly.

Our guide, Marwhala, accommodated us at her home after her duties were over; another household of mourning females offering delicious food and fascinating conversation. One of the younger women admitted bashfully that she was attending a consciousness-raising class. Even in this forgotten corner of old Europe modernity can't be kept completely at bay.

We walked in the mountains with our hosts, breathing alpine air and finding wonderful berries, nuts and mushrooms. I was asked to visit the uncrowned king of Mestia, the local priest, Father Gyorgy. At first he refused to talk to me because I was not wearing a long skirt, but he later relented.

He told us more of the history of the Svanetian people who claim descent from the Sumerians and practice customs dating back to the ancient Greeks. This was the land of the Golden Fleece and even today local people still sacrifice bulls and eagles alongside Christian rituals. Suddenly, Father Gyorgy changed the subject.

'Is it true you have a queen in your country who is over one hundred years old?' He said his wife was eager to know about the royal family. The wife smiled shyly from the kitchen as she prepared coffee for us. With her long skirt and headscarf she could have been a Muslim woman rather than the wife of a priest.

It was reputed that the Amazons came from Georgia, living along the river Terek. Remembering the old ladies with their rifle I was willing to believe this.

'Tell people to come here; we need tourists,' pleaded Father Gyorgy. I suggested gently that more modern plumbing and fewer kalashnikovs might be an inducement. He dismissed this notion with a wave of the hand.

'The plumbing we can arrange, the gun problem is not as bad as it seems.' I laughed nervously as he promised to take me up to Ushguli, Europe's highest inhabited village on my next visit, only five more hours on atrocious roads but quite mind-blowing, according to Tina.

'Come again,' urged Marwhalla; 'bring chocolate,' she added wistfully. 'We can't get it up here.'

I left for the mammoth drive back to Tbilisi and the flight home. There must be something in the thin mountain air that causes people to develop in a certain way. The characteristics of the Svanetian people can be found in other parts of the world where the mountains form the backdrop to tumultuous lives.

The doughty Edith Durham found this to be true when she travelled in the Balkans at the beginning of the twentieth century. In her book *High Albania* she faithfully chronicled the strange ways and lethal habits of the people. A song from the Balkan Peninsula would serve as well for the Svanetian region.

Oh we're back in the Balkans again,
Back to the joy and the pain-
What if it burns or it blows or it snows?
We're back in the Balkans again.
Back, where tomorrow the quick may be dead,
With a hole in his heart or a ball in his head-
Back where the passions are rapid and red-
Oh, we're back in the Balkans again!

Edith travelled in men's clothing, cut her hair short and often slept rough. The local tribesmen refused to believe she was a woman. Miss Durham chose to take this as a compliment.

On the flight home I remembered fondly the two grannies offering to scrub my back in their tin bath while commenting on the general uselessness of men who were only interested in fighting.

It will be some time before Georgia becomes a regular tourist destination. It is not a country for the faint-hearted but it holds treasures for the intrepid traveller.

7
India - The Wheel of Life

At ten pm on a Friday in late November I boarded a Gulfair flight to Delhi. I had finally achieved a life-long ambition to see India. Like most of my generation I had been raised on the stories of Rudyard Kipling, now dismissed as politically incorrect. At school I had been friends with an Indian girl whose reminiscences of her homeland added to my longing for the East. I have always had a craving for the exotic and the colourful, for the places where the world is wild and strange.

I sat with my luggage on a London tube train heading for Heathrow wearing the most colourful and inappropriate (for November) items of clothing I could assemble, anticipating a landscape and a culture as different from my own as I could imagine.

The plane was crowded and I was the only Western woman on board and one of the very few women, apart from the stewardesses who, I noted, were all blondes and wore little veils attached to their hats.

I had a middle seat between an elderly Indian gentleman and a young Arab who looked annoyed when I ordered a glass of wine with my meal. Unfortunately, the malaria tablets started to kick in and I threw up the entire meal while the two men slept. I managed to vomit neatly into a bag which I stuffed hurriedly under my seat. From then on I felt very fragile and drank only mineral water.

There was a long stopover at Bahrain where the desert heat enveloped me in a breathless hug when I stepped on to the tarmac. I wandered around the huge duty free airport admiring the gold jewellery and expensive cars on display.

As I drank Seven Up in the café I gazed at the runway simmering in the blazing desert sun while the local men paced up and down the air-conditioned walkways dressed in spotless white robes. I regretted that I couldn't reach India by way of a long sea voyage with its opportunities for reflection and intrigue.

The plane had emptied out quite a bit when we re-boarded for the short hop to the fabled city of Muscat in Oman. From the air the white walled city gleamed by the deep blue waters of the Gulf. Only a few years ago this city was completely cut off from the modern world. The Sultan travelled around in a Rolls Royce pulled by his loyal subjects. Now they have a soccer team and the players were boarding the plane in full kit, waving camcorders, en route to play against Abu Dhabi. I managed to doze off despite the noise.

We landed at New Delhi in the evening after a journey of about ten hours that seemed to have lasted for a week. I collected my bag and went in search of my messenger. Fortunately, I spotted him easily, a bearded gentleman with a turban and a bad cold. He grabbed my bag and hurried me outside to where an ancient taxi waited.

India hits you broadside immediately: heat and dust and exotic smells, noise and chaos, rickshaw taxis, hooting and shouting. We set off at speed along the airport road in the gathering dusk only to grind to a screeching halt as a cow wandered sedately through the traffic.

Between sniffs the driver told me a horrifying story about a coach full of tourists that ran over and killed a cow somewhere in rural India. The locals dragged the driver out and beat him to death while the terrified passengers looked on. I didn't feel immensely cheered by this tale but the driver obviously enjoyed it. Forty minutes later we arrived at the Connaught Palace Hotel, a thoroughly luxurious, insulated slice of Western life designed to ease the transition into Indian culture.

By the time I had unpacked, showered and settled myself it was past midnight. I had the room to myself for one night until my room-mate and the rest of the group arrived.

I was woken by a strange cracking sound early next morning and when I opened the blinds I saw a small hockey pitch under the window with some locals getting in an early practice session.

During the morning the other members of the group arrived in relays. The group leader was a young English woman and the travellers were from everywhere - Australians, Canadians, Scots, Dutch and Belgians, two Londoners, myself and one American woman, my room mate, who had not yet arrived.

There were several people my age but most of them were thirty-somethings, seasoned travellers fresh from trekking in Nepal. Even the seventy-year-old Belgian woman sported a T-shirt saying that she had white water rafted. I felt like a wimp in comparison, but even Isabella Bishop had to start somewhere. I had succumbed to pressure from my family and abandoned solo travel temporarily in favour of joining this group.

That evening we went en masse to eat at a local restaurant frequented only by tourists and wealthy local businessmen. We had an excellent meal enlivened by the sight of a large, black rat running under the table and across the room. We speculated on whether it was just passing by or visiting relatives in the kitchen.

At one o'clock in the morning I was roused by the arrival of my room mate. Far from entering quietly she made a point of shaking me awake so that she could introduce herself. I grunted a few words and fell asleep again.

Early next morning Peggy gave me a condensed version of her life story and urged me not to feel shy with her. I was not quite sure what she meant but I assured her that I was fairly unshockable unless she practiced strange rites involving human sacrifice or suffering to animals. I had forgotten that Americans don't care much for irony. My room-mate bolted into the shower at this point and I went down to breakfast alone.

After a shaky start Peggy and I got on quite well. We considered each other to be deeply eccentric and left it at that. On that first day together we made our way to a nearby bank and attempted to change some travellers' cheques. The crowds inside the building behaved as if tickets for a cup final or a pop concert were at stake. There were no women in sight and a great deal of ogling of my companion's bare legs went on. I had elected to wear linen trousers.

The tellers obviously understood what we wanted but did not take our requests seriously. We obediently visited offices on various floors obtaining a collection of stamps and signatures. Everything was recorded in ancient ledgers and apart from a few telephones there were no signs of the IT revolution. It all seemed like a re-run of a 1940s film, which I would have found fascinating if we had not been made to feel so unwelcome.

Later we tried to change money at the hotel desk but the same bizarre scenario took place. The throng of men around the desk occupied the male desk clerk exclusively. If he was aware of our presence he didn't show it. It is the norm here for women to be served last, if at all, but we were naive enough to imagine that our status as Westerners made us honorary men.

Peggy was seething by the time we were finally served. I waited for the full frontal feminist attack but she accepted the money sullenly and left remarking that the service was lousy. Only the beggars made no distinctions on grounds of gender.

Banking must have changed little in India; another Victorian traveller, Marianne North, also had problems.

I was nearly at the end of my money, so I went to the bank (there was one on Coutts' list), showed my letter and asked an old gentleman there if he would give me some money. He read the letter of credit slowly three times and said deliberately,

"It cannot be done."

"Why not?" said I.

"Because it is a most irregular proceeding." So I wished him "good morning."

Ever philosophical, she went to borrow fifty rupees from the Head of Forestry.

Later that afternoon a courtly Sikh gentleman, Mr Singh, arrived to show us around Delhi. The Lutyens designed buildings housing the government offices and the Parliament were enormous red sandstone sprawls originally designed to emphasise Britain's imperial grandeur. We moved on to Gandhi's tomb and the lotus shaped Bahai temple. Multi-coloured crowds buzzed around everywhere, the women in their saris like gorgeous, red, blue and gold bees.

At the Red Fort snake charmers and acrobats demanded fifty pence to be photographed and the female gardeners giggled hysterically at Peggy's mini skirt. An obliging cow pulled the municipal lawn mower in the grounds of the Fort. Her driver also demanded money for a photo opportunity. Inside the sprawling red sandstone palace the bare courtyards and rooms were gloomy and melancholic, emptied of the luxury and the teeming members of the Moghul Emperor's court. Perhaps the melancholy had seeped into the red walls; many of the former ruler's household were virtual prisoners there.

Emily Eden, an indefatigable chronicler, attended the King's court with her brother, the Governor General, in 1837. She noted that;

There are hundreds of the royal family of Delhi who have never been allowed to pass beyond these walls and never will be. Such a melancholy red stone notion of life they must have!

A number of female travellers in India and the Middle East wrote eloquently of their visits to harems and their meetings with the hapless females in their gilded prisons. Usually, the reality was far removed from the romantic imaginings of men.

Dusk was falling by this time and I remembered that I had not applied insect repellent before leaving the hotel. When I told Mr Singh that I could hear the whine of mosquitoes he assured me they were 'Making music only.'

As I was bitten on the ankle I resigned myself to malaria and a plague of hideous tropical diseases. Peggy claimed that she had natural immunity. When I expressed scepticism she explained that she had Tartar ancestors and she lived in Florida. I suppose no insect would dare to bite a descendant of Genghis Khan. Throughout the trip she laughed at my nightly fussing with mosquito nets and creams. She would have slept with the windows open if I hadn't insisted on closing them.

We returned to the hotel to pack ready for our journey on the Jodhpur Mail Express at eight thirty pm. As we were struggling to the elevators with our bags - or rather with Peggy's bags and my modest grip, a messenger arrived to tell us that the train was running several hours late.

When we finally arrived at the station the train was waiting but showed no sign of leaving. We were not allowed to get on board and we leaned against our mountain of luggage while the life of the station carried on around us. Vast numbers of people appeared to live permanently on the platforms, occasionally shoved aside by uniformed staff when passengers arrived.

The young Belgian in our party tried to intervene when a small shoeshine boy was savagely beaten around the head by a guard. The boy was preparing to clean our dusty sandals. He scooted off into the dark recesses of the platform but emerged later when the guards had gone. Rats ran among the bodies sitting and lying around us and men visited child prostitutes under the stairways; little girls with the faces of old women. I reminded myself that child abuse existed in Britain too but the thought did not comfort me.

When we finally got aboard it was almost dark and we settled into our compartments for the night. Peggy and I shared with the elderly Belgian couple who were pleasant but not very exciting company. Peggy immediately burrowed into her sleeping bag with a book. She regularly went to bed at seven pm throughout the trip, which led to speculation about her real motives for travelling. The group whiled away several late hours over G and Ts discussing this. Peggy had dropped hints about her husband's religious mania, which seemed a good enough reason to me. She had been everywhere from Tbilisi to Tobruk via Outer Mongolia, always retiring to bed at seven p.m.

I didn't see her eat any meals during the trip. She had a bottomless supply of dried emergency rations, protein bars and herbal teas on which she sustained herself. Her precautions and my luck enabled us to remain upright when sixteen of our party of twenty were laid low with Delhi belly.

I decided that eight o'clock was too early for bed, especially on the hard bunks of the Jodhpur Mail. After Peggy had settled herself with a paperback and a protein bar I watched as the Belgian, Georges, tenderly tucked his much older wife into the top berth. During the trip he fussed over her as if she was a rare jewel. I didn't think such husbands existed any more. Ashamed of my cynicism I left in search of more stimulating company.

Further along the carriage assorted Aussies, Canadians and Scots were having an impromptu party. Some bottles of wine were produced and poured into tooth mugs and a friendly Indian army officer travelling to Jodhpur joined the party as we noisily exchanged tall travellers' tales.

Outside, the profoundly black Indian night slid past the windows. Occasionally, we would see a wavering blue light near the track that gave glimpses of people huddled around cooking pots in shacks open to the sky.

An hour or so passed and the train came to a juddering halt. The sound of heavy boots was heard in the corridor and two armed and disapproving officials looked into the compartment. I couldn't determine whether they were soldiers or railway employees but they were energetically arguing with our guide about 500 rupee fines. Apparently it is illegal to drink alcohol on Indian trains - or possibly they made up the rule on the spot

After an angry exchange they went off and no money changed hands. Ruth, our guide said that they were trying to supplement their wages in the time-honoured way. We congratulated her for fending them off but the party broke up after that and I wandered back to my compartment. Peggy was still reading and the Belgians were asleep.

Before creeping into my sleeping bag I was forced to visit the toilets. The Indian officer had told us that both eastern and western facilities were available. The eastern version proved to be a hole in the floor and the western toilet was too horrible to even consider. A hole in the floor it would have to be.

After a chilly and restless night our steward brought us "bed tea" and a splendid Anglo-Indian style breakfast. He pulled the covers off the dishes with a flourish revealing omelettes with curried potatoes. There were always curried potatoes for breakfast in India. The train rattled along at what seemed like a steady ten miles per hour. By the time we arrived in Jodhpur it was midday and the temperature had climbed to 30 degrees.

Most of the old Rajput palaces in the city have been turned into hotels by their owners. Our lodgings were in cottages planted in a wonderful garden full of lushness and colour and vivid tropical creatures. We encountered the occasional gentle-eyed cow on the winding paths and handsome young men in orange turbans hovered outside each cottage waiting to fetch and carry for us.

This luxurious life would last for only twenty four hours; our real purpose in Jodhpur was to visit the fabled Mehrenagarh fort before leaving by bus for the Great Thar Desert.

We climbed up the huge hill to the fort at the hottest point of the afternoon, almost getting sunstroke on the way. Mehrenagarh is huge and overpowering, inducing awe and longing in equal measure. Founded in the 15th century it remained the stronghold of the local ruling family until the Union of India in 1949. The city of Jodhpur sprawled out below and from the battlements of the fort we watched a magical sunset with a huge orange globe setting low over the city and the vivid blue roofs of the Brahmins' houses.

Kipling wrote that Mehrenagarh was so vast and impregnable that it must have been the work of angels, fairies and giants ....*no man yet has dared to estimate the size of the City they call the Palace, or the mileage of its ways.* The fort was a mysterious and moving place full of secluded harem quarters for the women and mosaic-encrusted rooms displaying jewelled howdahs and carriages. The saddest sight was the wall covered with the imprint of female hands, a last gesture made as the women went to the funeral pyres of their husbands to be made suttee. Many of the palm prints were child-sized.

A few of the early British women in India were fearless travellers and endlessly curious about their adopted country at a time when the Raj was still establishing itself. Later in the 19th century codes of conduct, especially for women, became more rigid and the memsahibs withdrew from the real India as far as possible, preferring to create a tropical version of the Home Counties.

Fanny Parkes travelled around the country in the 1830s and 1840s with just a couple of servants, endlessly amused and intrigued by the sights, sounds and smells of the sub-continent. It was rumoured that her husband, an official in Allahabad, went mad during the cold season, *"so she says it is her duty to herself to leave him and travel about."*

Fanny resolved to immerse herself completely in Indian culture; she learned Farsi and Hindi, played the sitar and wrote about everything she saw. She was equally at home watching dancing girls, collecting information about Thugs or enjoying the food. Completely without inhibitions, she gossiped with the ladies of the zenana, smoked opium and assisted at Indian weddings. Striking up an unlikely friendship with the ex-Rani of Gwalior, she entertained the ladies of the court with demonstrations of riding side-saddle. Observing some Hindu religious practices she was "*Much disgusted, but greatly fascinated.*" In a later age Fanny would have been a fine anthropologist.

By the end of the nineteenth century such behaviour on the part of English women was regarded as both bizarre and offensive. The colonel's wife who wrote under the pen name of Lawrence Hope became notorious not merely for her sensuous and disturbing poetry and stories about India, but also for her total immersion in the life of the sub-continent, its languages and culture, its costumes and philosophies. Was Lawrence Hope (Adela Florence Cory) simply over-romantic and a lover of purple prose, *"Pale hands I loved beside the Shalimar"* etc, or was she one of those people who identify totally with a country not their own? The Portuguese have a saying that the place where your spirit fell to earth is the place that exerts the most sway over you. That spot is not necessarily the place where you were born.

There was just time to take a photograph of some schoolgirls in bright red and white uniforms that looked identical to the one my daughter had worn in Bristol. These little relics from the days of the Raj occur in unexpected ways. Then it was time to return to our cottages in the hotel garden to pack for the journey into the desert.

8
"For the Red Gods call me out and I must go!"
Rudyard Kipling

Jaiselmer must be the most magical and Kiplingesque sight in the Great Thar desert. Several hours hard driving in our ramshackle bus brought us to Prince Jaisel's 12th century sandstone city, with its towers and bazaars and network of alleyways sleeping in the sunlight. Once a caravan stop for traders leading camel trains burdened with silks and spices and opium, it seemed as amazing to us as it must have appeared to those medieval merchants. Only the motor scooters hooting around the alleys struck a modern note - and the shopkeepers who came out to ask us did we know their cousin Ashwin who lived in Leicester?

Unloading our bags in the courtyard of the Jawahar Niwas palace, the Maharajah's servant directed us into the shadowy foyer. Another impoverished Rajput prince had turned his home into a hotel offering a glimpse of Victorian British India among dusty palms and old military portraits.

As palaces go, the Jawahar Niwas was small; a series of apartments around sun- bleached courtyards. The prince himself lived in a top floor apartment well away from the tourists. He kept a large hound that ran up and down on the ramparts howling in the small hours. The building was less impressive than many Victorian municipal buildings in England but full of odd corners and unexpected delights. Old clocks made in Birmingham, their rusted workings untouched since the 1920s, ornate mirrors covered with a fine film of desert dust and creaking peacock chairs in gloomy corridors, fascinated me.

As usual, my roommate and I had drawn the short straw in the accommodation lottery. We were allocated what appeared to be the broom cupboard off the main corridor while the others had spacious quarters in the former harem, the zenana, in rooms full of mosaic tiles and mirrored archways.

Of course, the beds were old and creaking and there was no water but we were not in Jaiselmer to sleep and one of the elderly attendants obligingly brought us a bucket of hot water for washing.

If we had been around in Marianne North's day we would have been introduced to the Maharajah. The ruler of Jaipur sent his largest ceremonial elephant to her lodgings so that she could paint the animal in the garden.

He was covered with crimson and purple velvet heavy with silver embroidery...Two golden lions were sitting on top of his head, his face was covered with silver plates and bells, while on his ears dancing girls were painted. I wanted to paint him kneeling down, but he moaned so much over the cramped position that I let him off.

Marianne's paintings and sketches can be seen in the North Gallery at Kew Gardens in London. Like Isabelle Bird she was a late starter as a dromomaniac, but after the age of forty you could say that she travelled for England. The paintings were the most important result but her journals also make lively reading. Her sensibilities were of the time; she described how she hid behind a rock as a local ruler went by in procession. She did not feel like giving away her sketch *"To a half civilised human being I had never seen before."*

Later, in the open-air restaurant across the square, we discovered that water was liquid gold in this place. All around us in the spice scented air the rosy desert light faded showed the outlines of the sandstone houses and squat watch towers, cracked and lop-sided. The town is crumbling away, sinking into the desert sands just as that other fabled city, Venice, is crumbling into the waters of the Adriatic - and for the same reason. The stresses of increased tourism and modernisation are destroying this ancient place.

Within living memory the water of Lake Galigat was the sole source of supply for the few thousand inhabitants. Then a modern water system was piped in followed by a small but steadily increasing trickle of tourists. More shops and restaurants were opened, travel businesses sprang up and the pressure on the water supply grew and grew. The sandstone citadel's foundations began to soften as the water level dropped. A monsoon a few years ago aggravated the problem.

A third of Jaiselmer's historic buildings have fallen down and many others are unsafe, festooned with warning notices. The city is now on the UN list of the one hundred most endangered sites of historic interest. This is India, however, and things change slowly if they change at all and this fairy tale spot may yet disappear into the sands like Nineveh and ancient Tyre.

Next day we wandered around the medieval alleyways admiring the Havelis, the 17th century houses built by rich merchants. The façades of these three and four storey buildings were elaborately carved and coloured, their fretted windows and graceful balconies designed to enable the women to see out but not be seen. They would be very suitable material for fairy stories featuring djinns and genies and dark eyed maidens waiting to be rescued by warriors riding out of the desert.

Kipling's Kim would have been at home here, stealing sweetmeats from the bazaar and shouting in the rear of a Hindu wedding procession, even though Lahore was Kim's stamping ground, not this little desert fortress.

In the streets the women were eye-popping oases of colour in fuchsia and saffron with every bauble they could find hung about them. They held naked brown babies and gazed out at the passing world, the wandering cows, little black goats and the woman selling toe rings near the main gate of the citadel.

Here in this magical place grim reality can still intrude. The Indian army tests it nuclear weapons in another part of the desert.

While we were wandering around Jaiselmer I had not glimpsed any camels but I knew there must be plenty of them in the offing. We were due to leave on a three day camel safari - an event I was anticipating with mixed feelings.

I have always had doubts about camels: elephants, fine, but never trust any animal that sneers habitually. I was about to discover that camels had several habits far worse than an attitude problem.

We walked into the camel park at the edge of Jaiselmer where about thirty animals were waiting with their drivers. The men all started to wave and shout, urging us to choose their particular camel. By the time I had collected my wits the only one available was the tallest beast with the worst sneer and the youngest driver. I had a bad feeling about this. I was the shortest person in the group, the camel was the height of a small apartment building, and the driver looked all of fifteen years old. Peggy was already mounted up and demanding to be photographed. I was told that the camel's name was Johnny Walker.

'This animal is doing anything for me,' declared the fifteen-year-old, whose name was Akim.

'That's nice!' I smiled nervously.

Johnny Walker showed no inclination to kneel down and let me mount up. Akim shouted several times and waved his whip threateningly while the camel snorted and began to implode, its knees buckling gently and the rest of its body crumpling like a deflated hairy balloon. Its sneer remained intact. A certain Victorian lady, the Hon.Impulsia Gushington had better luck in Egypt.

My heart bounded with joy; I had always wanted to try the paces of a camel...

My camel knelt obediently for me to mount, but dismounted me again in the act of regaining its legs. However, I soon learnt how to arrange my position so as to ensure security and a certain amount of comfort...my camel proved to be gentle, easy and docile. I found myself often slumbering in its rocking motion......

In fact, Impulsia never existed; she was the creation of a witty Anglo-Irish aristocrat, Helena Selina Blackwood (Lady Dufferin) who wrote a spoof travel book lampooning the witterings of over-enthusiastic lady travellers. This was *Lispings from Low Latitudes (1863,)* a rare but coveted example of a witty, acerbic send up of the genre. The book contains a wonderful illustration of a mad-looking female at full gallop on a camel, hair and skirts flying in the breeze. I knew that I secretly aspired to this look but I was falling far short of my own expectations.

I clambered onto the uncomfortable saddle, clutching for dear life as the camel reared up and I found myself staring down what looked like the Cresta Run without the ice. The ground seemed very far away as Johnny Walker reluctantly followed the other animals that were already some distance down the road heading for the desert.

For the next three days Johnny tried to remain in the rear, showing a marked preference for the other direction, always heading for home if possible. Akim appeared to have no control over the beast. I suspected that he had not gained his NVQ in camel maintenance, or whatever was the local equivalent.

Down in the Valley of the Kings Impulsia rhapsodised over the countryside:
Our course lay for some hours at the foot of low, undulating hills sprinkled with gay bushes of the castor-oil shrub and the deliciously scented yellow mimosa; while on the right, large fields of sweet lilac vetches and patches of tobacco in full flower, stretched downwards to the river.

Someone would appear from nowhere with cold drinks whenever we stopped for a rest in the desert. Sometimes there would be a shack containing just one large, ancient refrigerator powered by a generator. The camels sucked up vast amounts of water at the wells and we had a chance to stretch our legs. By the end of the safari my legs were bowed and the smell of camel permeated everything. I was beginning to have renewed respect for Lawrence of Arabia.

The Thar came into its own at night: by day the camels plodded through sand and stony ground interspersed with scrub and the occasional grim, breeze-block settlement where hordes of children would appear, jeering at the camel train and demanding money.

When we stopped to visit a small temple a notice forbade menstruating women from entering. The two Canadian girls in the party were so outraged they urged us to boycott the place. The children, our chief hazard, were thankfully under control in the next village where they were lined up ready to give us a concert. Their teacher drilled them like mini-soldiers and they obliged with a few verses of "My bonny lies over the ocean." I wondered what the concept of the ocean meant to these little desert dwellers.

I went into a village house with our guide. We had been invited in to sit cross-legged on the bare floor of the cave-like dwelling. There were a few cooking pans, a sleeping area and little else. Pictures torn from magazines adorned the concrete walls, mostly of Hindu deities and Bollywood stars. I asked about the Thar;

'Too hot!' the women chorused. They were proud of the fact that the son of the house was receiving schooling. An exuberant eight-year-old he was delighted with the school bag our guide had brought from Delhi.

The male Canadian member of the group was still suffering badly from a version of Delhi belly. His daughter fed him antibiotics but his condition worsened to the point where he had to be tied onto his camel. Our guide said there was no hospital within reach and if there had been we would not have wanted to use it. Occasionally, the sick man lay prone on the sand while his daughter fanned him.

As night fell a transformation took place. After we left our belongings in the tents and aired our damp bedding we watched the camel drivers, now metamorphosed into cooks, prepare the evening meal over campfires.

Johnny Walker had a leg hobbled by a peg in the ground, his sneer mercifully hidden by the velvet blackness of the desert night. The men sang as they cooked, a harsh, mesmerising chant, as the mystical emptiness of the desert wrapped itself around us. The stars had never seemed larger or closer to earth.

After the meal we sat around the campfire as the sound of drums and cymbals grew louder and a quartet of nomadic entertainers moved into the firelight. The woman dancer gleamed in pink and gold, her anklets and bracelets jingling. The men were wild-eyed as they chanted and played. The leader of the camel drivers told us that the group came from the Kanjar tribe of nomads - untouchables, of course. The woman also doubled as a prostitute, he added helpfully.

As the singing and drumming grew more frenzied people got up to join in the dancing. In the background a camel snorted. Suddenly, as suddenly as they had come, the group melted away into the desert.

I returned to my tent and lay in the sleeping bag thinking of the strangeness of India and its many gods and cults. As a child I had read my grandparents' encyclopaedia and learnt a great deal about the cult of Thuggee, aided by the various lurid films on the subject.

During the early days of the Raj the British made determined attempts to stamp out the practice and the word slipped into everyday use back home. With typical insouciance Emily Eden, sister of the Viceroy, described

how, after visiting a Rajah's country palace-
We came home to breakfast and to rest, and the gentlemen went to the prison to see some Thugs. You may have heard about them before, a respectable body of many thousand individuals, who consider it a point of religion to inveigle and murder travellers, which they do so neatly that "Thugee" had prospered for two thousand years before it was discovered. A Captain G here is one of its great persecutors officially, but by dint of living with Thugs he has evidently grown rather fond of them, and has acquired a latent taste for strangling....
India can have a strange effect on Europeans.

On the final day Akim decided that Johnny Walker must be made to gallop. The other camels galloped occasionally and the boy felt that he was losing face by his inability to control the animal. Up to that point he had contented himself with pestering me for cigarettes and I had almost adjusted to the camel's uncomfortable gait.

'We don't need to gallop,' I protested, but Akim pointed in the direction of the disappearing group and shook his head.

'Faster!' he shouted, shaking his whip at the beast which turned his head around and bared his teeth in a ghastly grin. This seemed to enrage Akim who started beating the animal around the head with the whip until it must have seen stars. Johnny W stopped in his tracks, sucked in his cheeks and spat a huge gob of spittle straight into the unlucky youth's face.

I huddled behind Akim's back in a cowardly fashion wondering what Lawrence would have done in the circumstances. The last of the camel train was disappearing over the horizon and I was stuck in the middle of the desert with a truculent quadruped and a bolshie teenager who was by now almost incandescent with rage. He screamed at the camel at length in the local language, no doubt casting aspersions on its mother's virtue. After a few more heavy beatings the animal suddenly shot forward without warning and took off at great speed, almost throwing both of us onto the sand.

There is nothing more unpleasant than galloping on a camel. The effect on the kidneys is embarrassing and any spare flesh jiggles around in a painful manner. I yelled at Akim to stop but he had forgotten me. Transformed by the speed factor he continued to urge Johnny on like a Derby day jockey. It was just my luck to throw in my lot with a boy racer. We caught up with the others and passed them as they cheered us on. For a brief moment we were in the lead until Johnny got bored and came to a full stop, producing several loud farts. At the end of the day when we made camp the drivers had a camel race for our amusement. Johnny Walker came in last.

As we trailed back into town at the end of the safari we passed three Australians on bicycles heading for the Thar.

'You can't cycle in the desert!' I called to them.

'Anything's better than riding one of those f------ things,' they replied. I knew what they meant.

In 1850 Fanny Parkes wrote, "*Roaming about with a good tent and a good Arab, one might be happy forever in India.*' I think she was referring to a horse.

9
Travellers' Notes

I was just the latest in a long line of British women who had been entranced by the desert, if not exactly enamoured of camels. Female travellers started to visit desert lands in the 18th century, mainly accompanying spouses and male relatives. Whether travelling from choice or necessity, the impact was the same.

When the first English consul was appointed in Libya, to the court of the Bashaw of Tripoli, his family, including his unmarried sister, accompanied him. Miss Tully kept extensive journals during her ten year stay.

She became an intimate of the royal family, recording scenes of barbaric cruelty as well as exotic harem life and the wonders of Roman Libya. Life was cheap at the Bashaw's court, especially the lives of women and slaves. In order to reach the ruler's harem Miss Tully had to follow a eunuch along dark, underground passages, through a great iron door where- *a striking gloom prevails. The courtyard is grated over with heavy iron bars, very close together, giving it a melancholy appearance. The galleries round the courtyard are enclosed with lattices cut very small in wood...and the great number of attendants filling up every avenue makes it almost impossible to proceed from one apartment to another.*

Despite these precautions intrigues and liaisons flourished, usually facilitated by slaves. Miss Tully recounted several highly coloured accounts before chronicling a famine in great detail. She was a punctilious observer whether describing mourning customs or the appearance of the city after the plague, the rigours of a thirteen month quarantine period, a plague of locusts or the arrival of pirate ships in the harbour.

Civil war broke out between Moors and Arabs and the Tully family had to rely on the kindness of the townspeople who were well-disposed towards them. Despite all of this Miss Tully continued to describe the fantastic clothing of the people that delighted her eye and the grandiose weddings at the royal court.

The Tullys' long sojourn in the desert came to an end when the Bashaw was deposed by a Georgian adventurer who insisted that the European representatives should approach him barefoot. This was too much for the English to tolerate: war, pestilence and famine were one thing but lèse majesté was quite another. The consul and his family returned home.

During the 19th century a procession of hardy British women followed each other across various deserts and many settled there for long periods. The uniquely eccentric Lady Hester Stanhope made the desert the backdrop for a tempestuous and almost unbelievable life. She wore male Eastern costume, lived in a remote fortress in the Lebanon, took lovers openly and consorted with religious prophets, rulers and weirdos of all kinds. She befriended the Druze and was well acquainted with the various factions that still divide the Lebanon today.

Eventually, she became addicted to the local drug, the Datura flower and became a religious crank. Expecting the Mahdi to arrive any day, she would ride away with him to usher in a new world order. Instead, she died alone and poverty stricken in her ruined castle where her decomposing body was discovered weeks later among dozens of feral cats.

In addition to unstoppable Englishwomen like Isabelle Bird, a small number of European women became great travellers. In addition to Alexandra David Néel, the Frenchwoman who explored Tibet, there was the Austrian Ida Pfeiffer and Alexine Tinne, a wealthy and beautiful

Dutch girl - a true dromomaniac who longed to reach the centre of Africa. She traced the source of the Nile but she was murdered in a particularly gruesome manner by Tuareg tribesmen in the Sahara. The modern advice to travellers to avoid conspicuous displays of wealth was ignored by Alexine. She was believed to be carrying a hoard of gold and paid for it with her life.

By the time she died in 1863 she was alone; fever having carried off her maid, her doctor and her intrepid mother who accompanied her everywhere on a white donkey equipped with a padded backrest and a parasol. Travelling light was never a necessity for wealthy Victorians. The Tinne entourage included a grand piano so that Alexine could play Chopin under the desert stars.

Isabelle Eberhardt was definitely the wildest and most eccentric of the European women who fell in love with the desert. With her mysterious and romantic origins – she was the illegitimate daughter of Russian nobility - her conversion to Islam and her rejection of a personal fortune in order to embrace a life

Most of the 19th century travellers were glad to return home, at last, when old age and infirmity overtook them, despite their hatred of the British climate and the Victorian way of life. Only Margaret Fountaine died in harness, still catching butterflies in the Caribbean aged seventy two.

The Passionate Nomad, however, spent the last years of her life disguised as a man, riding around the North African desert, spying for the French, marrying an Arab soldier, suffering from malnutrition and drug addiction. In her own mind she was free and perfectly well;-

How can one explain the fact that at home where I had warm clothes, an outstandingly healthy diet, and mummy's idolatrous care, the slightest chill I caught would degenerate into bronchitis; whereas here, having suffered freezing temperatures at El Oued, and at the hospital as well, having

travelled in all kinds of weather, while literally always getting wet feet, going around in thin clothes and torn shoes, I don't even catch a cold? The human body is nothing, the human soul is all.

It was a strange irony that she was to die soon after in a flash flood in the desert, aged twenty seven years.

Gertrude Bell was the most influential of the desert queens. Eberhardt and Lady Hester Stanhope were dismissed as weird, if colourful women, but Bell became a powerful figure and a founding figure of the new Iraq, forged after the First World War. Because she was deemed to have the brains of a man the British Government found her very useful as an envoy to the Arabs and an adviser. She spent years among the Arabs and founded the Museum of Antiquities in Baghdad that suffered so much in the recent war.

Her words have a sad, ironic ring in the light of that country's present sufferings. She loved what she saw as the romance of that area, the two great rivers, Tigris and Euphrates, the huge stretches of desert that once were fertile and blooming - the Garden of Eden - and the awesome antiquity of the place.

Lifting her long skirt and clutching her hat, swatting the black flies and mosquitoes, Gertrude took in the houses in old Basra made of yellow brick, their latticed, wooden balconies leaning out over the teeming streets. She wrote to her father: *I feel as if I were in my own country once more and welcome it, ugly though it is.*

The last of the Victorian lady travellers, one whose expeditions were made well into the twentieth century, was Freya Stark. Another woman mesmerised by the desert, Freya came from an unconventional background. She lived most of her life in Italy when not travelling through the Middle East. She was one of the finest travel writers of the century and certainly her work stands head and shoulders above most other accounts of the last one hundred years.

Like Gertrude Bell, she worked for the British Government for a while, supplying invaluable information during the Second World War.

Her books with their splendidly evocative titles, *Dust in the Lion's Paw, The Valley of the Assassins, Alexander's Path*...describe a part of the world where the life she saw has vanished for ever under the heel of progress, oil wells and war. Like Edith Durham she was given the status of honorary man by the nomads she met.

The Viennese traveller, Ida Pfeiffer, also resorted to masculine disguise when necessary. In China she decided to walk around the walls of Canton, a feat which no woman had ever attempted. She was only able to do this in disguise, accompanied by a European missionary. Feelings against Europeans were running high at that time.

We passed through a number of narrow streets paved with broad stones. In every house we saw in some niche a small altar, from one to two feet high before which lamps were burning; the quantity of oil wasted in this way must be enormous... as in the Turkish towns, each trade had a street to itself, the dealers of glass in one street, the silk merchants in another...the life and movement in the street were very great, especially in those where provisions were sold. Women and girls of the lower class were walking about, making their purchases as in Europe. They were all unveiled and many waddled like geese; for as I have before observed, the custom of crippling some of the women prevails in all classes.

All these little streets were built along the wall; and all doors, closed in the evening, lead into the interior of the city which no foreigner dare profane... Except Ida, of course, who rose to every challenge.

Rosita Forbes was also at home in the Middle East at the same time as Lawrence and Gertrude Bell. In her more matter-of-fact way she described her love of the desert to Sayed Idris in Benghazi-

I told him how I loved the desert and how, like the Emir Faisul, I was happiest when, from narrow camp bed, I could look at triangle of starlit sky between the flaps of my tent. "I too," said Sayed Idris, "cannot stay more than a month in one place. Then I must move on, for I love the smell of the desert."

It is true; there is a scent in the Sahara, although there may be no tree or blade of grass for a hundred miles. It is the smell of the un-trodden earth.

Rosita became well-known after she made a gruelling and dangerous crossing of the Libyan Desert in search of the lost oasis of Kufra or Kufara, then sacred to a tribe called the Senussi who were hostile to foreigners. She was the first woman and one of the very few Europeans to have made the journey.

She planned it meticulously; learning Arabic and the Koran, disguising herself as a Muslim woman and calling in every favour from her distinguished acquaintances. It was a time when Britain still held sway in that area and Rosita was based in Egypt.

Her description of the hardships suffered by the expedition members was chilling. The survival of the group depended on the camels and the girbas – goatskins treated with oil and tar so that the water they held always tasted unpleasant. The ration was one pint per day.

I lived month after month as an Arab and a Muslim. I consorted only with desert men, hard, loyal and superstitious. Gradually, I learned to know them. They were a strange mixture of courage and fears, of wisdom and childish simplicity. They were witty; coarse and chivalrous to a veiled woman, vastly endearing, beset by all manner Of crude doubts, but unwavering in their spiritual faith. As we travelled at the slow pace of a baggage camel – rarely more than two miles an hour – further and further into the desert, I became part of the small, isolated brotherhood represented by our caravan.

They were starving, smothered in sand, attacked by hostile villagers, covered in lice, footsore from seventeen mile marches and maddened by thirst. On the return leg of the trip things were even worse. Only four people remained; her main companion was badly injured and they left a trail of blood and pus in the sand until they were rescued by a British camel train sent out by Lord Allenby. It is always good to have friends in high places.

Rosita's best selling book about her journey, *The Secret of the Sahara*, made her name. Why did she do it? The journey is its own reward. Kufra is about as far as one can get across Libya. Today the journey can be made by four wheel drive and the information is available on a website.

Women travellers of the nineteenth century may have been seduced by the romance of the desert but they also attempted to conquer mountains at a time when women simply did not do that sort of thing. Of course, mountaineering also required a large retinue.

A French aristocrat, Henriette d'Angeville was the first woman to climb Mont Blanc in 1838.* Her luggage contained a feather boa, a black velvet mask, a friction brush, a shoe-horn and a pigeon in a cage. Her clothing weighed twenty one pounds and consisted of a voluminous belted cloak, fleece lined, peg top trousers and thick woollen stockings over silk stockings. A close fur trimmed bonnet was on her head with a green veil and a matching long black boa, black velvet mask and deep fur cuffs.

Her only special equipment was an alpenstock, but there were six guides, six porters, a mule driver and a mule (unused). It's encouraging to note that this proud Frenchwoman wore English flannel next to the skin. Her three day expedition was successful and she boasted of it in her book, *My Ascent of Mont Blanc...*

"Three days which my friends like to refer to jokingly as The Great Days of my Glory!
Following these events, I indulged myself in the pleasure of a bath, and when I emerged from it, I felt so well that I was almost inclined to embark on another ascent!"

* A French girl, Marie Paradis, was the first woman to reach the summit of Mont Blanc in July 1808, but she was carried unconscious for the last few metres owing to altitude sickness.

10
Ranekhpur-Pushkar - Karma

The Jain temple of Jaya Sthamba at Ranekhpur could lay claim to be the Chartres of India were it not for the fact that the sub-continent is littered with magnificent temples and religious monuments. The Jains in particular were responsible for some of the greatest religious architecture over the centuries.

Among them reverence for life is taken to such lengths that the life of a devotee or renouncer revolves around avoiding the destruction of life in any form. The diet of a Jain must be purely vegan. Most followers live a much less severe version of the religion and are among India's wealthiest merchants.

The chief priest of the temple was waiting to greet us at the main door under the fluttering prayer flags. Aged about thirty five and with the face of a medieval saint, he wore an orange dhoti and nothing else. He explained the basic philosophy of the religion in simple, fluent English:

Jainism is one of the most influential minor religions in India with about four or five million followers. Mahavira, 'the Great Hero' trad.599-527BC is considered to be its founder. He is also referred to as *Jina* or spiritual conqueror from which the word Jain is derived. The religion is divided into two sects of whom the digambaras or sky-clad Jains are the more ascetic version. I had seen one of the sky-clad Jains on the road to Pushkar.

Their main belief is that every living thing contains a soul or spirit. It is therefore difficult for a truly religious Jain to eat anything at all. Some of the digambaras will starve themselves to death in old age in a specific ritual. I was so fascinated by this information and its similarity to the Cathar heresy in 13th century France that I almost missed the equally interesting news that the only Jain temple outside India was in Leicester.

The priest waved his arm gently at the magnificent interior and commented that the building of temples was considered an act of religious merit-just as it was in medieval Europe. Before leaving us and graciously accepting an offering for the temple, the young saint (as I now thought of him) emphasised the non-violent core of Jainism. For this reason the temple would be regularly and gently swept so that insects could not be trodden on by the pilgrims.

He led us into the building and left us to wander around. Ranekhpur was huge with vistas of arched walkways and carved niches occupied by shining black idols; their crystal eyes following you as you walked past. The white marble and stonework was carved with a riot of tropical flowers, animals and birds interlaced with scalloped edged balconies. Supporting pillars were carved in the shape of a ceremonial elephant- no two are alike.

Arch upon arch, level upon level, the temple soared up nine storeys to the carved towers or sikharas topped with finials. At ground level bells tinkled and pilgrims carefully washed and anointed the statues, decorating them with garlands of orange marigolds and jasmine flowers, burning incense and leaving offerings of food by the twinkling lamps.

They barely glanced our way as we tip-toed around the columned halls in our bare feet, inhaling the perfume of tropical flowers and what must have been the centuries old odour of sanctity-far stronger here than anything I had experienced in Europe.

I noticed that the shrines to Lakshsmi the goddess of wealth and Sarasvati the goddess of wisdom were particularly well attended. The priest had told us that in another part of the temple there was a vast library or bhandara, filled with richly illustrated manuscripts. We were not invited to see these, although the writer in me would have loved a glimpse. The goddess Sarasvati is invoked by scribblers.

Nowhere have I felt so indescribably in another world as I did in Jaya Sthamba. As I emerged into the blinding sun and searched for my sandals I had for one second the sensation of landing on earth from another planet. I wished I could have spoken longer with the priest about Karma, which I believe is a kind of genetic essence. I would have appreciated some advice about my own essence.

Outside on the dusty, arid plain in front of the temple stood a woman begging-hardly an unusual sight in India, but this woman was the tiniest, most bird-boned creature I had ever seen. For a moment I thought it was a child until I saw her wrinkled face. Only in this country can such people be seen-the result of generations of semi-starvation. I wondered if she was a Jain; their women are required to fast frequently. Jain theologians, like their Christian counterparts, once debated whether or not women had souls. For the female of the species - east or west the karma is the same.

In the lovely palace-fringed city of Udaipur I found the only fat baby in India – at least, the only one I saw during my trip. He was the son of a silversmith who was putting together a necklace for me consisting of black beads, blue lacquer and a silver medallion of the goddess Parvati. It was a far cry from Emily Eden's egg sized emeralds, but I was delighted with it. The fat baby sat on his mother's knee wearing only an amulet and a big smile.

Later, as I wandered around the City palace, now a hotel as well as the Maharajah's home, the ruler himself arrived in his Mercedes, greeted with deference by the staff. The India of the princes may have officially disappeared but they still command respect in Rajasthan.

From the boulevard in front of the palace we gazed out

across Lake Pichola towards the fairy tale white building that is now the Lake Palace Hotel. The palace was once given as a dowry to the Maharanis of Udaipur. It is now a popular venue for wealthy honeymooners.

That evening we took a boat across to the palace to enjoy a cocktail in this exquisite location. Sitting on a terrace full of shimmering mosaics and marble tiles enhanced by coloured lamps and bright starlight, I thought of the closely guarded queens who spent their summers here. It epitomised the luxury and sensuousness that is part of India. The queens were long gone and I had lived well over half my life. Lawrence Hope, the lover of all things Indian, knew this feeling when she wrote,

The years go hence, and wild and lovely things,
Their own, go with them, never to return.

In Jaipur, the pink city, I didn't see a grand ceremonial elephant but I had the opportunity to do the tourist thing and ride on one of the great beasts up to the Amber Fort. I had heard that the animals could be unpredictable – sometimes actually causing the death of a tourist – but I was impressed by the laid back attitude of the mahout or keeper of my chosen elephant. As the creature ambled along the highway breaking off large branches and eating the leaves, one of the tourists on board complained about the slow pace. The mahout, appalled by this example of tourist crassness glared, shook his head and said 'Elephant having breakfast!' In other words, get off and walk, you fool.

Jaipur is famous as a centre for jewellery making and I bought some tiny stones after wandering around an emporium filled with dazzling examples. We stayed in a small guest house with restful gardens where we ate wonderful tropical fruit in the vegetarian restaurant. It was close to one of Jaipur's most famous sites, the Hawa Mahal, or Palace of the Winds. Built with more than nine hundred of small, lattice windows, the design enabled the women of the zenana (harem) to watch the world unobserved and also to allow free passage of air through the building.

The journey to Pushkar was a leisurely ramble through Rajasthan punctuated by encounters of a satisfyingly Asian kind. The sight of a sky-clad Jain holy man at the side of the road, his body smeared with mud and ashes reminded me that I had first read of such people when I was eight years old. I knew that the piece of gauze across the man's mouth was to prevent him from accidentally swallowing an insect such is the religion's respect for life.
As the bus passed him he did not look up; India is India and buses are too recently arrived to be of importance in the scheme of things.

We had already stopped briefly at a pilgrim's rest house by a large and beautiful lake - an improbable sight in this parched province. Dignified, bearded men sat on the terrace overlooking the water, tapping their curved slippers and nodding their orange turbaned heads to the beat of a Hindu melody played on someone's transistor. We drank cold drinks and anticipated Pushkar, a beautiful and very holy place according to the pilgrims.

Along the roads we saw Rajasthani women in their orange and fuschia veils bowed under heavy loads of wood and anything else which needed to be transported. Men were never seen carrying anything. They worked in the fields driving the water wheels or tractors while their womenfolk toiled in the sun. It was in this area that a well-documented case of suttee had occurred in the 1980s. Nobody had been punished for this illegal and horrendous burning. Most of the villagers believed it had been a good thing that had brought blessings and prosperity to the area.

Pushkar is famous for its camel fair (mela) held in November - the largest of its kind in the world. The area around the little town is covered with a huge tent city; the event attracts hundreds of tourists as well as people from all over India.

On a day to day basis Pushkar is one of the country's most sacred Hindu sites with the only temple to Bramah in the country. Built at the foot of a holy mountain, the town spreads around a sacred lake fringed with ghats. Small guesthouses overlook the water and we stayed in one of them, relaxing on the veranda next to an asthmatic fan and dusty potted palms.

As the sun went down and small lights twinkled in the town we were surrounded by amplified hymn singing. This went on at all hours: I found it hypnotic and quite restful but some of the group admitted to being driven crazy by the sound. Having been to Lourdes and being accustomed to Gregorian chant it all seemed fine to me and quite normal for a pilgrimage centre.

In the evening we went out into the town in search of a meal and discovered that Pushkar also has a reputation as a hippy centre-or former centre now that those glory days of the sixties are over. A few elderly, sandal wearing types from the West were noticeable in the open-air restaurants and everyone was getting mellow with a little bhang - a yoghurt drink flavoured with marijuana leaves which is legal in India.

The waiter obligingly explained that there were three strengths of bhang and he would bring us number three. Some of us knew what we were getting but a few innocents in the party were completely unaware. We all downed several glasses of mango flavoured bhang with our meal and it was only as we started to weave our way back to the guest house that the effects were noticeable.

I was pleasantly high and found myself at one point lying on the veranda on top of the parapet with a sheer drop into the holy lake below. Naturally, I found this very amusing and I went on lying there until the person in the next room came and hauled me back. Pushkar has a dusty, laid back charm of its own but the effect is heightened by several glasses of bhang lassi.

Next morning I went out into the bazaar to buy my fix of Indian textiles. At the barber's booth I was invited to have my hands painted with henna in the traditional manner for good luck.. The barber said his sisters would do it. We arranged that I would come back at two thirty and he would take me to the house. On the way back to the guesthouse I was followed by a saddhu - a holy beggar rattling his bowl. He followed me up to the door and would probably have followed me inside if I hadn't given him something. It is unthinkable to a saddhu that anyone would refuse him alms. It is a religious duty for Hindus.

After a short siesta under the fan I was back at the barber's booth ready for my beauty session. The barber led me into a maze of back streets empty in the afternoon heat except for emaciated dogs and the occasional monkey. The accommodation consisted of very small concrete blockhouses with steps at the side leading to the upper floor and roof space. The windows were open to the elements and I saw no sign of electricity.

Inside the house the barber introduced me to his sisters, two tiny girls who seemed no older than twelve or thirteen, but both were married and one cradled a baby. They wore colourful Rajasthani kilts and nose rings and crouched on the floor offering me the only chair in the room. There was no furniture, just a few rugs and cushions.

The girls placed the baby on a cushion and set to work. As they painted elaborate patterns on my hands they cross-questioned me in pidgin English. Was I married? Where was my husband?

'At home' I said, not wanting to get into a discussion about divorce which is almost as big a disgrace as widowhood in India. I was not asked how many children I had, only how many sons. I said one and they looked relieved. They pointed proudly at the baby, 'Boy, very good!' they exclaimed. Attitudes do not change quickly in India and Rajasthan remains medieval in its attitude to women.

I remembered Emily Eden's description of a child Ranee, eight years old-The little queen was –

...something like a little transformed cat in a fairy tale, covered with gold tissue and clanking with diamonds. Her feet and hands were covered with rings fastened with diamond chains to her wrists and ankles.

I sat in the sun allowing the henna to dry before returning to the guest house. The girls waved me off, clutching the money and the infant. On the way back I stopped at the tailor's booth to ask about more textiles. The tailor showed me a chart on the wall that explained his lineage. He belonged to the tailoring caste as his ancestors had for centuries. I wondered if he ever dreamed of becoming an engineer or a poet.

Back at the guesthouse the hymn singing was louder than ever and everyone complained of headaches. One person had climbed the holy mountain with the pilgrims which met with general approval. Clutching a colourful puppet I had bought on my way back, I explained about my henna expedition.

This was taken as further proof of my eccentricity. The Dutch social worker refused to sit next to me at dinner when she saw my hands, saying that it was unhygienic. I thought her attitude was amazing in the late twentieth century and not so different from that of Emily Eden, describing her visit to the harem of the Rajah of Benares in 1836.

They carried us through a great many courts, and then the Rajah gave me his cold, flabby little hand, and handed us up some narrow dirty stairs and came in with us behind the purdah and introduced us to the Ranee, his mother, who was very splendidly dressed, and to some of his sisters, who were ugly.
Then they asked us to go and see an old grandmother, and

*the Ranee laid hold of my hand, and one of the sisters took F., and they led us along an immense court on the roof to the old lady, who is blind and very ill; but they dressed her up for us, and we had to kiss her, which was not very nice.
....When we came back to the Ranee's room, she showed us her little chapel, close to her sofa, where there were quantities of horrid-looking idols - Vishnu and so on.*

The hymn singing seemed to be building up to some sort of climax. I lay on my bed for a siesta soothed by the chanting while Ruth complained of feeling feverish and others begged for ear plugs. I felt they were not getting into the spirit of the place.

I looked at the souvenirs I had placed at the end of my bed-a Rajasthani puppet, a silk shawl and some mirror - work cushions. I could probably have bought everything in Camden Market in London but it wouldn't have been the same.

Emily Eden at least had the satisfaction of bargaining for cashmere shawls before they were imported wholesale into England as well as being offered a king's ransom in jewels.
*Such jewellery as we saw yesterday morning! A native was sent by one of the gentlemen to show us some really good native jewellery. There is an ornament called a surpeche which the rajahs wear in their turbans, but there is seldom such a handsome one as this man had for sale. It was a diamond peacock holding in his beak a rope of enormous pearls, which passed through an emerald as big as a dove's egg; then there came the tassel- the top was of immense diamonds, with a hole bored at one end of them, and they were simply drawn together into a sort of rosette, without any setting. Then there came strings of pearls, each ending in three large diamonds.
They stick it into their turbans with a gold hook, and the tassel hangs over one ear.*

Emily added a nonchalant postscript to this-

We have steamed quietly along today, and I have been asleep half the afternoon.
I liked her style.

11
Daspan-Varanasi - Desert Days

The village of Daspan is unlikely to appear on many maps, but this mall, dust-shrouded hamlet in the Thar Desert, well away from the tourist circuit, offered us the warmest welcome we had received in India. Visitors were rare in this isolated area and the general absence of Western tourists meant that no screaming hordes of children awaited us demanding rupees and sellers of souvenirs and rolls of film were conspicuously absent.

The reception committee consisted of the entire village lining the streets to applaud our arrival. The town's taxi service was drawn up in anticipation – three bullock carts. We embarked on a triumphal tour of Daspan which is home to the Rabari and Bishnoi tribal peoples. Twenty minutes earlier we had arrived at the 'big house,' Castle Durgan Niswas, owned by the local Rajput lord.

'Just call me Michael.' He was a slim, handsome man wearing the most elegant jodhpurs I had ever seen. He walked around with a transistor radio clamped to his ear, giving us a running commentary on the India v England test match.

The house was furnished in the typical 1920s Raj style but creature comforts were few. The remote community relied heavily on goods being trucked in from distant cities. The effects of the latest drought were in evidence. Indra, the god of rain, had been making fewer and fewer visits. Michael was worried that there would be nothing very much for dinner that evening, 'Except rice, of course.'

Undeterred by this possibility, we set off around the village making obligatory visits to the bow and arrow maker

and the silversmith among others. I watched as a heavy, carved silver bangle I had chosen was carefully weighed and recorded. At the house of the bow
and arrow maker the women of the family posed for photographs, giggling and jostling, clutching babies and trying to keep their veils across their face. They were very intrigued by the women in our party, our short hair and trousers.

'Are they really women?' they asked our guide.

I longed to get my hands on one of the long fuschia pink veils worn by Rajasthani women. By the time I left India I had accumulated several items including a turquoise and gold silk sari. I didn't intend to wear these items but they were covetable souvenirs. The sari would grace my bedroom window for a long time back in England.

The choice of appropriate clothing occupied women travellers of the past even more than it does today. Modern women's magazines advise taking miniature versions of your favourite toiletries and packing heated rollers so that you can look presentable on the beach. Victorian women simply took most of their household and wardrobe, adding a few extras for the tropics.

The wealthy American traveller, May French Sheldon, always took a long, white sequined gown, a flowing blonde wig and lots of sparkly jewellery to impress the locals. I'm sure the women of Daspan would have appreciated such a show on our part. Sheldon travelled in Africa with an entourage of one hundred and thirty five retainers, but few travellers of that time were really alone; alone meant without another white person.

Back at Michael's house dinner was served on the flat roof with a view of desert starlight and fireworks popping to celebrate a marriage in the village. As our host had predicted, the meal was mainly rice and lentils flavoured with spices, but Michael mixed cocktails for us and told us stories of his illustrious warrior ancestors. Descended from an ancient and impeccable lineage, from princes who kept cheetahs and peacocks at their court and a harem of hundreds of veiled women, he was now an innkeeper and acting bartender for wandering Western tourists. Soon after, he left to check on the test match and a couple of servants cleared away the plates. I was relieved that the local aristocrat did not have to do the washing up.

In bed that night I looked at the guide book trying to establish exactly where we were in the Thar. I read about the fabled golden city of Tonk, the only Muslim kingdom in Rajasthan, once famous for its library established by a former ruler. It sounded as if Tonk was now a very run of the mill town, definitely not on the tourist trail. As always I was thinking ahead, anticipating the next horizon like a true dromomaniac, although I could happily have stayed longer in Michael's little town, despite the culinary shortcomings.

Isabel Savory, travelling in India at the end of the nineteenth century had written-

'Too often travelling is a fool's paradise. I am miserable, I want to get out of myself; I want to leave home. Travel! I pack up my trunks, say farewell, I depart. I go to the very ends of the earth and behold; my skeleton steps out of its cupboard and confronts me there. I am as pessimistic as ever, for the last thing I can lose is myself; and though I may tramp to the back of beyond that grim shadow must always pursue me.'

This was depressing reading; I doubted that Freya Stark and other female travelling titans had beaten their breasts in that fashion. I noticed that Peggy was already asleep under her various layers. I closed the book and turned out the light.

Before we left Michael's house I told him about my aversion to camels and how much I was looking forward to seeing some elephants like the one described by Marianne North. He told me that for certain festivals elephants were

decorated and painted and were a magnificent sight,
 'Like geisha elephants!'
If elephants are now an impractical way of getting around, cycling continues to be popular despite the state of India's roads. At the turn of the twentieth century a tough American traveller, Fanny Bullock Workman, was cycling seventy miles in one day in the tropical heat. She must have been an improbable sight at that time. Unlike most of the women in the small, exclusive band of globetrotters she travelled with her husband, but her achievements were still remarkable. She set world records for women mountaineers as well as cycling virtually around the world. In her day, at least, the monkeys had not been spoiled by tourism.

On this day we sat under a spreading tamarind tree to eat our tiffin. Shortly half a dozen rather small, dark brown monkeys climbed into the branches over us, and watched us attentively. At last, one more adventuresome and perhaps more intelligent than the rest, cautiously descended, and sat on a small branch about ten feet above us. After a few moments he began to open and shut his mouth rapidly, looking directly at us, evidently intending to indicate that he wished for some of our food. As we did not appear to notice his appeal, to emphasise it and to show us he was in earnest, with an expression of great determination he seized the branch with both hands and shook it several times much as an excited child might do. Was not the karma of that monkey about fitted for its next transmigration into a human being?

My own experience with monkeys had been very different. They were so used to being fed by tourists that they snatched any food from our hands as soon as it appeared.

When we arrived in India's holiest city it seemed, at first, like any town in any state with chaotic traffic, run down shops and beggars on the sidewalks, until, in the distance you catch a glimpse of the mighty Ganges and the red and gold temple roofs shining in the sun.

The bus slowed down at a red light, an unusual event in itself, and suddenly, the stump of an arm covered in rags was thrust through the window inches in front of my face. A leper had spotted a good business opportunity- a bus full of western tourists.

I jerked back momentarily, my skin crawling, but before I could find a coin the bus moved away and the lepers were left waving their stumps in the air. One woman obligingly lifted up a child who appeared to have elephantiasis for us to see. By this time we were becoming, if not hardened, almost accustomed to these sights. Inevitably, this happens in a place like India.

When we met our local guide he told us that Varanasi was the place where every good Hindu wanted to die, if possible. It is a combination of Lourdes, Rome and Jerusalem. The town is full of hospices for the dying, many of whom take on a new lease of life in this heady atmosphere. They linger on for many months while their relatives beggar themselves to pay the bills - much like England, but we lack the spiritual advantages. It is believed that this spot has a direct line to the next world, a conduit to eternity. If a person dies here, he or she will slip effortlessly into Paradise, including foreigners and unbelievers, our guide assured us. He also told us that it was impossible to die in Varanasi "If it is not your time to go… no matter what happens to you.' Of course, we were not able to test the truth of this boast.

Our guide walked us around the city down narrow alleyways often ankle deep in water and streets thronged with shoppers and pilgrims. Some of us begged for a pause and a cup of tea but we were not allowed this until we had arrived at the river bank to see the burning ghats, the place where funeral pyres are lit. Mr Patel pointed at the remains of one such pyre.

'They must have been poor people; they did not use enough wood or sweet oils.' What looked suspiciously like a thigh bone protruded from the ashes. Some people in the party turned green and hurried away. Our guide smiled knowingly, 'Would you like to stop and take a little bhang?'

We sat in a tearoom overlooking the red-roofed monkey temple and the golden mosque which was surrounded by armed guards. Tensions between Hindus and Moslems were running high. Pilgrims scurried around and the sick were being carried in litters towards the river. Men sat around us chewing betel nuts, displaying red-stained teeth.

We were awaiting the highpoint of our visit, setting out by boat to see the dawn rise over the Ganges. Mr Patel again led the way as we emerged dazed but expectant at five am next day.

He led us to the boat in near darkness and we were rowed into the centre of the fast flowing river. Even at that hour pilgrims were on the banks washing and brushing their teeth in the brown water in which human remains and dead animals floated. The dhobi wallahs were beating clothes against the stones as we threw the traditional flowers and floating candles onto the tide. I resisted the impulse to trail my hand in the water but Mr Patel assured us that no-one ever caught a disease from the sacred mother of all rivers despite the unbelievable levels of pollution. Seeing our doubtful expressions he scooped up some water in his hands and swallowed it.

'The water is not as dirty as it looks; as you can see, I am in the best of health!' he grinned cheerfully. The Australian nurse in the party raised her eyebrows into her hairline as we watched in fascinated horror.

Gradually, we fell silent as streaks of light appeared in the sky. The ancient palaces and hospitals built by the maharajahs over the centuries began to shimmer in a pale blue haze. We sat still and breathless, listening to the gentle swishing of the oars on the vast expanse of water, enveloped in that ethereal light. As the huge orange ball of the sun appeared, poised between the horizon and the river it was easy to believe that this spot was a stairway to heaven.

Mr Patel murmured a prayer as we watched the sun climb high in a sky now ablaze with pink and gold. The dark brown river was also turning to gold as the flames of the first funeral pyres rose into the air.

One hundred and fifty years ago Emily Eden was not quite so impressed although she admired the architecture of Benares, as it was formerly known.

... and the s*tone is such a beautiful colour. The ghats covered with natives (sic), and great white colossal statues of Vishnu lying on the steps of each ghat. Benares is one of their most sacred places and they spare no expense in their temples.*

Her party landed with the usual herd of elephants and two or three hundred baggage camels, a sight unlikely to be witnessed these days. When the Governor General met the Rajah of Benares their combined processions of elephants and camels blocked the city's narrow streets completely and everyone was forced to walk. The ruling British moved around in great processions often covering less than fifteen miles in a day. The size of their entourage and the gifts of diamonds, rubies, pearls and sapphires lavished on them by the local rulers make eye-popping reading. One gift consisted of a bed with gold legs completely encrusted with rubies and emeralds.

The Lord Sahib's caravan boasted 850 camels, one hundred and forty elephants, hundreds of horses and bullocks and an entourage of twelve thousand stretching out for ten miles. Emily described it all with enthusiasm, while complaining loudly of the heat and dust, the sleeping in tents, the bouts of malaria or "feverishness," and the frequent depredations of thieves and bandits who made off with everything they could lay their hands on.

The natural magic of the great river was far more

memorable to me than the mosques and temples, even the temple at Sarnath, the cradle of Buddhism. There was a general unwillingness to return to mundane sightseeing as we climbed into the ancient bus once more.

Sarnath was fairly close to Varanasi: Maroon robed monks rustled among bookcases and yogis performed handstands in the grounds on the spot where the Lord Buddha meditated under a banyan tree. As we walked up the driveway towards the beautiful temple complex a coffee-coloured cow settled down in comfort under a monument.

I sat on a boulder to do my own meditation for a few moments watched by an interested monkey on a nearby stone. Soon it would be time to leave India after my short stay. I had not seen a tiger in the Sariska reserve – they do not come down from the hills in the rainy season. I had not met the Dalai Lama in Dharamsallah; that would involve another trip. There was still Kerala and Pondicherry to see. As for the Himalayas and the little train from Darjeeling that my school friend described...four trips to India would be a minimum requirement.

Despite my determination to go it alone on my travels I was quite relieved that I had made my first expedition into India as a member of a group. This country can be overwhelming and sometimes obstructive to a lone traveller, especially if she is female. Now that I had gained a feel for the country I would be happy to make solo trips in the future.

I recalled our visit to Agra which illustrated my point. This city has been a tourist venue for so long that as in Venice its inhabitants have a deeply cynical attitude to visitors. Many people have commented on its unkindness and the general lack of hygiene. Marianne North suffered while she was there and most of our group were laid low after eating in one of the hotels. Peggy and I remained upright. I was baffled by my good luck; I had eaten from the same menu as everyone else. Peggy, as usual, had eaten nothing at all.

Excursions into the town to admire the palaces and temples and to buy silk were enjoyable despite the problems and the unfriendly faces. Above all, the chance to see the Taj Mahal made everything worthwhile. It was worth crossing oceans to behold that white marvel, especially by moonlight, even if you were in a throng of people.

Strangely, the image of Agra that stays in my mind is the sight of the mighty River Jumna seen from a palace rooftop, with a turbaned, barefoot man in the distance herding water buffalo. Rivers and roads fascinate me the most. These are the homes of the gods and the real venues for all true dromomaniacs.

12
Interlude- In the Footsteps of Agatha Christie

After the overwhelming assault on the senses and the imagination that was India, the next stage of my travels was completely unplanned. Serendipity was at work here. I had taken a quick trip on the Hoverspeed service from Dover to Calais during a weekend visit to Kent. On my return, clutching my duty free purchases, I tore off the special portion of my ticket and gave it to the young woman in the scarlet uniform. She told me that the ticket would be entered into a competition.

'You could win a trip on the Orient Express!' she smiled.

'And pigs might windsurf,' I thought, before forgetting the whole thing. I was planning the next stop in my itinerary when a letter arrived from Sea Containers House in London telling me that my little ticket stub had led a charmed life. I was a winner in the competition and I could take a companion on the fabled train from Venice to London. We would be flown out from Heathrow and accommodated in a hotel overnight before boarding the train for the return journey.

I explained this to my friend Molly who was a fellow Venice lover. She spent several weeks in the city every year while her artist husband painted. I had also been a frequent visitor until poverty intervened. Molly was happy to accompany me and her husband assured us that he didn't mind staying behind.

Having decided when we would travel I put my other plans on hold and worried about the state of my wardrobe while re-reading Agatha Christie. I had nothing suitable to wear for such glittering surroundings and only a few weeks in which to beg, modify or buy a few outfits which would not disgrace me on my trip with the diamond-encrusted ones. After trailing around the world on a shoestring the thought of a journey with the glitterati, however short, was quite unsettling.

I met Molly at Heathrow: she was her usual calm, elegant self while I coped with my barely suppressed inferiority complex, even stressing over my luggage which didn't look sufficiently smart. We had made this trip so often; Alitalia jet from London, economy class, then the water taxi across the lagoon as the city rose out of the water like a mirage, a magical place of spires and domes from *A Thousand and One Nights*. Venice really does appear to float on the water as writers never tire of reminding us.

This time we sailed up the Grand Canal on a chilly but sunny afternoon with the sky full of scudding white clouds. The palaces and gondolas seemed, as always, to have come from a film set or a child's book of fairy tales. The great wash of summer tourists had gone and only a small autumnal trickle remained. For a few moments we had the water city to ourselves.

Then the steps of the station came into view and we walked a few yards to our hotel on the Lista di Spagna. A few hours of sunlight remained in which to wander around the alleyways, drink coffee and look up old friends. In the evening we went for a splendid fish dinner- a treat provided for us by Molly's husband.

Next morning we waited in the lobby of the Amadeus Hotel to be escorted to the train. With us were three other passengers for the Magic Puffa. They sat between the leather sofas and the gilded mirrors eyeing their mountain of luggage and looking morose. The two women wore mink coats thrown over their suits and excessive amounts of gold jewellery. The man wore gleaming leather from head to toe.

Molly and I looked anxiously at *our* luggage - one small case apiece - before wishing them 'Good morning'.

'Aye', they chorused in broad Scots accents before staring at their luggage once more.

At the station we were ushered into a cordoned off area in front of the train which sat gleaming in dark blue, red and gold on its special platform. Every door handle, axle and window was buffed and polished to perfection. I had never seen a train so eerily clean. I imagined legions of workers up all night preparing this prima donna of the tracks.

A group of Americans offered up their Vuitton luggage sets to be borne respectfully away.

'Don't worry!' whispered Molly, 'it's *new* Vuitton!' A crowd of well-dressed exuberant Spaniards followed us along the platform where the entire staff from stewards to chefs were lined up to greet us in impeccable uniforms. I thought I had slipped into a house party scene from a Merchant-Ivory film. I half expected to see a corseted Helena Bonham-Carter leaning out of a window.

Agatha Christie had travelled on the train often in its heyday and frequently used the setting in her crime novels, but I could find no record of any Victorian lady travellers making a trip on this train.

One woman, Annette Meakin, had been the first Englishwoman to travel on the Trans Siberian Railway soon after its inauguration in 1896. Like Alexine Tinne she dragged her long suffering mother along. They found that the luxurious carriages were fine at the beginning of the journey but standards fell as the days went by. In Siberia they were reduced to fourth class carriages, *"not a fit place for ladies; and English ladies too.'* I was sure that this would not be the case on the Orient Express.

Inside, our tiny compartment had everything we needed for the forty eight hour journey. I sat trying on the monogrammed slippers and playing with the toiletries while

Molly pretended not to notice my childish behaviour. We met our personal steward, a devastatingly attractive young Frenchman called Fabien who assured us that he was completely at our service. I thought wistfully of my vanished youth when I might have put his claim to the test. Instead, I checked the film in my camera.

The train was fascinatingly low-tech and I was overcome with nostalgia as I fiddled with lever operated windows and inspected the Victorian style toilets.

That night we made our way to the lounge bar to begin our initiation into the high life. The sleek Spaniards were making a lot of noise at the bar, occasionally breaking into V*olare,* accompanied by the official pianist who wore a green carnation in his dinner jacket.

The Americans, on closer inspection, seemed to be sinister Mafia types-hooded-eyed, sleepy looking Italian Americans, always smiling but with no style. They were accompanied by giggly young blondes.

Assorted nouveaux riche couples were settling down with magnums of champagne. There was a honeymoon couple in his n'hers Armani suits and a handsome young Irishman escorting a much older woman. She was quite plain looking but pert. He squeezed her thigh and massaged her bare ankle as they sat in the lounge bar.

'He's obviously a toy boy!' Molly whispered.

There wasn't a film star or a genuine aristocrat in sight, let alone Hercule Poirot. I remembered that even the cast of Eastenders had travelled on this train.

'And now we're on board,' Molly remarked. 'You can't keep the riffraff out these days.'

We sipped our champagne cocktails while I worried about the black chiffon trousers I was wearing. I had bought them the day before in Venice at a bargain price, but they were too long. Molly had shortened them using sellotape. I felt sure Agatha would not have approved. The British were noticeably less elegant than their continental counterparts.

This sad state of sartorial affairs must be a fairly recent one. When Lady Mary Wortley Montague was in Turkey as the wife of the British Ambassador she abandoned European costume whenever possible in favour of the Turkish costume which enabled her to wander around Constantinople unmolested. She sent detailed descriptions of her clothing to her friends in England and promised to have her portrait painted in the full regalia.

The first piece of my dress is a pair of drawers, very full, that reach to my shoes and conceal the legs more modestly than your petticoats. They are of thin, rose coloured damask brocaded with silver flowers, my shoes of white kid leather embroidered with gold.

Over this hangs my smock of fine white silk gauze edged with embroidery. This smock has wide sleeves hanging half way down the arm and is closed at the neck with a diamond button, but the shape and colour of the bosom is very well to be distinguished through it. The antery is a waistcoat made close to the shape, of white and gold damask with very long sleeves falling back and fringed with deep gold fringe, and should have diamond or pearl buttons.

My caftan of the same stuff as my drawers is a robe exactly fitted to my shape and reaching to my feet, with very long strait falling sleeves. Over this is the girdle of about four fingers broad...

This elaborate toilette was completed with a talpack – a cap of velvet and pearls or silver gauze with a tassel, and a cloak of brocade often lined with fur. Flowers and jewels were usually added to this ensemble. How I wished I could have worn such an outfit instead of the black chiffon trousers.

The morose Scots had overcome their fit of the glums and became more animated as the evening wore on and the champagne flowed.

'It's all right ye ken', said the man nodding at the bubbly, 'but it's no as guid as whusky.' His companions agreed and said the whisky could come later. I had already told Molly that I thought they must be lottery winners, and so it proved. They were market traders from Glasgow enjoying their winnings. They had no intention of giving up their trade which provided a livelihood and endless entertainment. The women assured us that you saw all human life in the market.

'Its fascinatin' hen!' the younger woman gave me a nudge in the ribs.

Soon we were in a procession into the dining car which was ablaze with shining silver and blinding white napery. Roses adorned our little table under soft pink lights. Gleaming walnut and marqueterie panels lined the walls and a small army of waiters placed exquisite and highly calorific food and wine in front of us. Whenever the train lurched wine and coffee would spill onto the pristine cloths.

Most of the forty eight hours were spent eating and drinking gargantuan meals with little snacks in between. I realised why the super rich were always checking themselves into health farms.

At night, in the comfortable but small bunk beds, the awkward clatter and roll of the train became more obvious. This was very old rolling stock, after all, despite the knock down glamour of its carriages. Soon after dawn the train stopped at a country station to take on fresh croissants for breakfast. Occasionally there was a brief station stop to allow the passengers to take some gentle exercise.

At dusk we sighted the Alps near Innsbruck. In the twilight the pinnacles turned blue and charcoal, shading into silver. Next morning we chugged slowly across France, watching from the observation lounge or chatting to the other passengers. Once I asked Fabien where in France he thought we might be. He gave a shrug of Parisian contempt.

'We are in ze sticks!'

Molly and I adopted our steward unofficially. He told us his life story and asked for career advice. He had worked on the train for two years and planned to go to New York for adventure. We were very nice ladies, he told us, simpatico, as they in Italian. At least he didn't say we reminded him of his granny. We tipped him heavily when we left.

Forty eight hours from Venice we were herded unceremoniously on to the cross-channel ferry with the great unwashed; no distinctions available here. We had said goodbye to the beautiful train but a smaller and slightly less polished version awaited us at the port.

A jazz band played as we boarded and champagne and petit fours were served. We asked our waiter what he thought of the passengers. This man was no Fabien. In strong estuary English he announced that they were all rich gits,

'Present company excepted, of course.' He added that it cost £2500 per person to make this trip. 'Criminal!'

The shock of arriving at Victoria station and having to take the tube was almost physical. Only the fancy labels on my suitcase and a copy of the Orient Express magazine remained as souvenirs, not forgetting the monogrammed slippers, the toiletries and several extra pounds in weight. I wondered if Agatha had faced this problem.

13
LA LA Land and Beyond

I left for Los Angeles a few days before Christmas on a crowded Continental flight that involved racing around Houston airport for a connecting plane. The girl sitting next to me had come from Eastern Europe to live in England. She had hitchhiked and taken trains to reach London and this was her first flight. She was going to visit her boyfriend in San Diego.

'I am not at all nervous,' she assured me as she sat twisting her hands. Meanwhile I was wondering how I would find California after an absence of more than twenty years.

My son and his girlfriend were waiting for me at LAX. Their apartment was on the quirkily named Descanso Drive which they translated as 'Chill out street.' Descanso was narrow, winding and full of bumps caused by exploding tree roots. The front door at Casa Descanso was flanked by large red lamps that made the building, nestling behind its screen of tropical foliage, seem like a hidden brothel.

The apartment was light and spacious with wonderful views. We drank red wine and ate Chinese food as we talked and talked until I suddenly crashed out with jet lag.

I awoke next morning to the sound of pouring rain. Everyone knows that it never rains in southern California so I must have jinxed the weather, as always. The girl friend and I went to the supermarket to shop for Christmas. Later we all went to Santa Monica to do gift shopping between showers. The famous beach seemed noticeably less glamorous in the rain.

On Christmas Eve I was driven around Hollywood's earthquake-stricken hills to admire the mansions of the stars.

Gate notices advised that "Intruders will be met with armed response." I tried to imagine that happening in England's stockbroker belt. We went to Venice, the small town down the coast that I remembered from the hippie heyday of the 1960s. People were skating along the beach road while crystal sellers and stargazers peddled their wares. Despite the laid back atmosphere there was an underlying feeling of menace in the place. At midnight the air was full of the sound of gunshots as the local Mexican population gave the traditional welcome to the Christ Child.

On Christmas Day we made the ritual calls home and my daughter in Edinburgh claimed that she was going to have a Chinese takeaway for lunch. I refused to feel guilty about this remembering all the years when I had twisted myself into knots in order to give my children a good Christmas holiday; the single parent syndrome in full bloom. My daughter admitted that she and her friends were hung over and the Chinese option suited them very well.

After an exchange of gifts we sat down to a turkey big enough for twenty. I congratulated myself that I had refrained from offering any cooking advice.

After Christmas one of the highlights of my stay in LA was a visit to the Huntington Museum, a treasure house of European culture transported to a mansion set in tropical cactus gardens. The collection included a Shakespeare first folio and Gainsborough's Blue Boy. We ate clam chowder on Sunset Boulevard and discussed my forthcoming trip. Near LA's splendid art deco railway station Mexican Indian dancers were performing in front of the old mission church of Los Angeles.

On New Year's Eve I bought a ticket and "entrained" for San Diego, a two and a half hour journey through fairly uninteresting scenery, but the train itself was hugely enjoyable, the carriages wide and comfortable and straight out of a 1940s Hollywood film. How boring our trains are in comparison.

At San Diego I took the local train called the trolley line to Chula Vista, a suburb which is the closest point to the Mexican border. The place has nothing else to recommend it to the visitor. I checked into a motel and spent New Year's Eve eating a take-away pizza and watching old Bette Davis and Liz Taylor movies. I had a telephone conversation with my son and spent another hour worrying about what my children are doing with their lives as opposed to worrying about my own.

Old friends from San Francisco arrived on New Year's Day, together with another couple and we set off for Tijuana, a typical border town full of noise, casinos, prostitutes and good, cheap eateries. Once it was simply a large brothel but the town is now filled with many pharmacies where North Americans buy their medicines at discount prices while arranging a visit to the town's cut-price dentists. Virtually any drug is available here at half price and without prescription.

Twenty-five years dropped away and I was back in the same silver shops and eating at Sanborn's restaurant. The friends were eager for gossip about the royal family and I obliged as far as I could, explaining that I was not a royalist.

Back in Chula Vista we parted and I had an invitation to stay in San Francisco at the end of my trip. After one more night in the featureless, noisy motel I took the trolley to the border, La Linea, and walked across the bridge from one country to the other. Walking is always the cheapest way to cross international boundaries.

I wasted some time trying to persuade both American and Mexican border officials to stamp my passport and provide me with the necessary permits. Eventually they obliged and I took a taxi to Tijuana airport for the flight to Mexico City. The flight was full and I was the only gringa on board.

Mexico City airport at seven p.m. was enormous, chaotic and seething with people, but my friend John was easy to spot, towering over the locals and as welcoming as ever. We took a VW beetle taxi miles across the sprawling city to the beautiful, historic suburb of Coyoacán.

John's apartment was on the oldest street in the Americas, Avenida Francisco Sosa, originally built by the conquistadors over the ruins of the Aztec City. I loved being able to stay in this tree-shaded slice of history with the sound of flamenco echoing across the old cobblestones from a local dance school.

John shared the apartment with his partner Jose Luis, who I immediately christened El Lobo, the wolf. I was introduced to their beautiful tortoiseshell cat called Pew. After dinner we chatted for hours and John gave me useful advice for my travels around Mexico. Jose Luis said he was writing a novel about his stay as a language assistant at Clifton College in Bristol.

Next morning I wandered around Coyoacán and visited Frida Kahlo's house which is now a museum. The house was a beautiful example of a Mexican villa with colourful tiles and Spanish colonial furniture, but there were comparatively few examples of Kahlo's work on display, more of her partner the muralist, Diego Rivera.

Coyoacán was filled with colour and elegance and history. The central square, the Plaza Hidalgo was always alive with music, buskers, balloon sellers, craft sellers and book stalls. The nearby church of San Juan Bautista, built in the sixteenth century had an almost delirious atmosphere of intense spirituality, an essence that I had felt in the Jain temple in India.

I lingered until the altitude and lack of oxygen made me so tired I was forced back to the apartment where I fell asleep for three hours.

'We thought we'd lost you,' was John's comment when I reappeared. In the early evening dusk we walked through the old Spanish streets to the modern part of the suburb. We shopped in the supermarket and he explained to me how to cook Nopoles (cactus leaves), a traditional delicacy.

The thick, juicy pads are de-spined, then either lightly grilled with oil or salted and chopped. They are often served at breakfast with eggs, being full of vitamin C. I spent a happy half hour admiring the staples of Mexican cuisine that are unavailable in the UK.

Later, we went to see a nostalgic film called *Garden of Eden* about the two-way traffic between Mexico and the USA; poor Mexicans going north in search of a better life (often illegally), and north Americans coming south in search of the "good" i.e. alternative lifestyle.

Outside the prosperous suburbs in the old colonial area Mexico City is chaotic, heavily polluted and overwhelming. Now the largest urban area in the world, it scarcely resembles the scene described by Madame Calderon de la Barca in the 1840s-

To me nothing can exceed the sadness of the aspect of this city and its environs-mountains of moving sand formed by the violence of the north winds, and which, by the reflection of the sun's rays, must greatly increase the suffocating heat of the atmosphere. The scene may resemble the ruins of Jerusalem, though without its sublimity. The houses seemed blackened by fire; there is not a carriage on the streets- nothing but men with the wide trousers slit up the side of the leg, immense hats and blankets, or serapes, merely a closed blanket; more or less fine, with a hole for the head to go through. The women wear reboses, long coloured cotton scarves, or pieces of ragged stuff, thrown over the head and crossing over the left shoulder. Add to this the sopilotes (vultures) cleaning the streets, disgusting, but useful scavengers...

John and Jose Luis told me that San Miguel de Allende was the place for me. Three weeks in a delightful, Spanish colonial town would be an ideal introduction to my Mexican travels. I could also brush up my rudimentary grasp of the language. In fact, I had already decided to go, if only to straighten out my confused thoughts about the town culled from reading guide books. The experiences of the travel writer Mary Morris in *Nothing to Declare*, and the views of an English author of horror fiction who hated the town and called it the Duke of Mantua's court, were mixed up in my mind.

Assuming that this was a reference to the opera Rigoletto, I had a jumbled picture of a place where local aristocrats seduced young maidens and then threw them into the river rolled in a carpet. This was crossed with a snapshot of an idyllic, if primitive town where your landlady's cockerel woke you at dawn and the neighbours were, if not actual villains, sufficiently rackety to give an edge to everyday existence.

It all sounded fascinating, if unlikely, and safe in my armour of the invisible middle-aged woman I thought that I could cope with any scenario.

John walked with me to the bus stop and waved me off in a collective taxi to the northern bus station. San Miguel was five hours away by road. During the drive through the vast, straggling suburbs of Mexico City and onto the super highway to the north I had plenty of time to think about my plans for the next few months and to reflect once again on my reasons for roaming the planet.

Most of all, I pondered on what it was in my nature that gave me a neurotic attachment to strangers and strange places; on what kind of thrill I got from being in far away places where I knew no-one, a kind of freedom, I suppose. That was something I shared with female travellers of previous generations. If travel is the saddest pleasure I would have my fill in the weeks to come, but only faint traces of melancholy afflicted me, never sadness. I had escaped, if only temporarily, from the problems of everyday life. I had come to be a wanderer among strangers, taking notes.

During the journey I read extracts from *Sister of the Road*, the autobiography of Box-Car Bertha who rode the railroads of the USA during the Depression years and lived as a hobo for most of her life. She also tried to analyse why women take to the road.

The women who take to the road are mainly those who come from broken homes, homes where the mother and father are divorced, where there are stepmothers or stepfathers, where both parents are dead, where they have had to live with aunts and uncles and grandparents....

That was not generally the case with Victorian lady travellers. Usually, they just wanted to get away. The forty five year old, middle class, Viennese Ida Pfeiffer wrote,

From my earliest childhood I have had an intense longing to go forth into the wide world. And she had no intention of taking a chaperone.

Her first sojourn abroad was described in *A Visit to the Holy Land, Egypt and Italy*. This was followed by a dismal few months in Iceland (cold and boring), before she set sail for Brazil in 1846. She spent nineteen months circling the globe, enduring numerous hardships, always plunging into the interior of the wildest jungles and meeting native people whenever possible.

Eventually her fame resulted in the Austrian government awarding her a small pension so that she could continue travelling. She often wore men's clothing and narrowly escaped being eaten by cannibals in Borneo. Only another woman was able to curtail Ida's wanderlust. In Madagascar the native queen, Ranavalona, believing that the Whites wanted to overthrow her, shut Ida in prison. After her release, the gruelling fifty day march to safety caused her to develop a tropical fever. She died in Vienna in 1858.

When I reached San Miguels's modern, Brutalist style bus station it was late afternoon I wandered up a hill towards the centre as the late afternoon sun glowed on the painted houses in the narrow streets, blue and rose, ochre and cream and custard yellow. Old men were leaving their seats in small parks and plazas and wending their way home followed by a tribe of stray, mangy dogs; local buses steamed out to the suburbs loaded with the workers.

I checked into a hotel called the Quinta Loreto, chosen at random from the guide book. I had been educated for a few years in a Loreto convent. The rooms formed a square around a courtyard garden. Mine was pleasant enough but the water was seldom hot. There were many elderly Americans there, wintering over. They would have preferred Florida but Mexico was cheaper.

After unpacking I wandered along to the main market area where stall holders were closing up for the day and eventually located the main square in front of the Parroquia, the magnificent church. The square was in fact a small, square park known simply as the Jardin rather than the Zocolo, as is usual in Mexico.

I sat down on a bench and took out my notebook to record first impressions. The Jardin was the meeting place for the whole of San Miguel and the main buildings in the town surrounded it on four sides. General Allende's house was next to the Parroqia and all the best hotels were nearby.

A visit to the Jardin would start my day during the following weeks, part of a well-trodden triangle of Jardin, library, casa de cultura. This was housed in a former convent with an exquisite courtyard and a café that served superb ice cream and coffee. Sitting on this patio, shaded by tropical plants, sipping coffee with a book on my knee and watching the sunset flaming over the cupola of nearby St Phillip Neri church was one of the golden moments of my travels.

Sometimes in the early evening the café would be almost empty and there would be no sound except the splash of the fountain and the discreet tinkle of spoons. After a final blaze of red and gold the sky would darken and it would be time to leave as the scars on the soul healed over.

I decided that I had no wish to be the modern equivalent of Box-Car Bertha. At heart she was too practical and too much of a realist for me. I fancied the role of a present day Passionate Nomad modelled on the unfortunate Isabelle Eberhardt...

My dissatisfaction with people grows by leaps and bounds...dissatisfaction with myself as well, for I have not managed to find a suitable modus vivendi and I am beginning to fear that none is possible with my temperament

Isabelle was only in her twenties when she wrote those words. I was still wrestling with this issue in my fifties.

I stayed at the Quinta Loreto for a few days before inevitably seeking out a cheaper lodging while, at the same time, arranging Spanish lessons. I eventually checked in to a semi-deserted hotel, this time very much in the budget category. Although quite near the centre La Huerta was situated in a small wood. The building had endured several extensions in its lifetime; balconies popped up unexpectedly and large public rooms gave way to small cell-like bedrooms. It was still very chilly at night and there was no heating. The place was eerily quiet and deserted. I met two German girls who left the following day and after that, no-one. Once I heard footsteps in another part of the building; these, combined with the bell that sounded mournfully at the gate from time to time, gave the place a decidedly Gothic atmosphere reminiscent of my stay in the haunted museum in Cordes.

I paid the tiny, black-clad peasant woman who sat by the gate in the mornings but when I asked about other guests she just shrugged indifferently. After a while the atmosphere began to get on my nerves. La Huerta was cheap but the strain of anticipating the footsteps of Count Dracula in the corridor was taking its toll.

After speaking to a vivacious, elderly lady who always wintered in San Miguel, I took her advice and went to a house on 27 Mesones Street. This was a small B & B in the centre, clean, welcoming and full of flowers. Two gay Canadians were just checking out and recommended the house warmly. When I told them about La Huerta they shook their heads in disbelief. There was a roof top patio where I sat watching the life of the town below as I washed and dried my hair.

The following day, Sunday, was so cold that I decided I needed a hot breakfast. I treated myself to a plate of American style pancakes and maple syrup in one of the best hotels. The dining room was full of the well-heeled down from Mexico City for the weekend. The rich are the same everywhere and so are their spoiled children. Most of the weekenders looked noticeably Spanish.

I went to mass at eleven am in the dazzling Parroquia - my first visit. The congregation was mainly devout Indians and Mestizos; the priest looked very Spanish. Still feeling at a loose end, I went for a large salad at café El Tomate. I had blown my food budget for the week in one day.

I was due to begin my Spanish lessons on the following day with a lady I met in one of the antique shops in the town. Dr. Lucia Tollis-Harbert claimed to be the widow of an English Earl and the daughter of a former Italian Ambassador to Mexico. After an extraordinary life she had settled in a cottage in San Miguel to a life of genteel poverty.

When I arrived at the casita I met the Lucia's two companions -a wolf and an Australian dingo. After a moment's shock at having a wolf jump up at me in a friendly fashion, I picked myself off the floor and opened my books. Lucia did not seem to find her pets unusual and so I decided I would be equally casual. As she told me more about her life I decided that she would need a whole novel to do her justice.

On January 17th the Blessing of the Animals took place at St Phillip Neri church. This traditional festival has been largely taken over by resident Americans who arrived with their Siamese cats and expensive dogs. Little Indian women in rebozos lifted up caged birds to be sprinkled with holy water. The proprietor of 27 Mesones told me that in rural areas people brought their pigs and goats for a blessing.

Lucia had been given special permission by the Mexican authorities to keep a wolf at home as long as she did not bring it onto the street. I was relieved that she had not brought Topo Gigio, the morose dingo, for a blessing. The elderly priest might have suffered a heart attack.

I wandered back to the house admiring the Christmas decorations shining and twinkling in the windows. Mexicans keep their decorations up until February 2nd-Candlemas, the official first day of spring.

I took a forty minute bus ride from San Miguel to Dolores Hidalgo for a return fare of sixteen pence. The town is famous these days for its tile and ceramic works. A network of small streets led into the market and the central plaza, which was larger and grander than San Miguels's. Its Spanish colonial church has a very photogenic façade but is less interesting inside.

In contrast to San Miguel there were very few foreigners to be seen on the streets. I came across some Americans in the tile factory I looked into. Despite lecturing myself about my lack of a house and a homeland thousands of miles away, I succumbed. Adorned with colourful cactus plants those tiles would later prove not be frost proof and would shatter in an English garden.

Dolores Hidalgo is a name that resonates in Mexican history. Every school child knows the name even if they are not sure where it is on a map. It was in this town in 1810 that the priest, Father Miguel Hidalgo, gave the rallying cry, the "Grito" which roused his countrymen to fight the war that would finally throw off the Spanish yoke.

I visited the house where Hidalgo lived as a parish priest and which is now a museum. There were some beautiful and moving tableaux showing the road to Independence which for the poor, at least, has never been fully realised. The famous remark by another Mexican leader said it all-

"Poor Mexico, so far from God, so close to the United States."

A group of polite, well-scrubbed school children in shining white shirts asked me where I was from. They were amazed to hear, 'England' having expected Canada.

'So far!' they exclaimed, 'larga distancia.' We talked about Hidalgo and Allende and the importance of "la libertad."

'Do many people in England know about Hidalgo and Mexico?' they asked. I tried to give a diplomatic reply but I feared the answer was no. Latin America does not figure large in the British consciousness and Mexico tends to mean a package holiday to Cancun. Not that the British are noted for their familiarity with anywhere abroad.

In 1717 Lady Mary Wortley Montague in her letters home from Turkey *(The Turkish Embassy Letters)* was berating her friends for this same ignorance.

*Your whole letter is full of mistakes from one end to the other......*She warns against inaccurate guide books...*They never fail to give you an account of the women which 'tis certain they never saw, talk of the genius of men into whose company they are never admitted, and very often describe mosques which they dare not peep into.*

Despite the overwhelming number of souvenir shops Dolores Hidalgo was more authentically Mexican than San

Miguel, more untidy, busier and ordinary. This must be due to the absence of resident gringos. The large, permanent colony of North Americans has transformed the face of San Miguel. It is now more aspirational, its shops westernised and its genuine Mexican ambience much diluted.

I was surprised that there were no souvenirs in the museum, not even a tasteful map of the battles of the War of Independence. It was all the more remarkable when the streets outside were full of tourist tat. San Miguel's tat was definitely better quality.

I was back in San Miguel in time to eat at Marco Pollo's café. As its clever name implied, the place served only chicken for travellers. The soup was very good but I had grown tired of budget chooks.

14
San Miguel-Guanajuato-Frogs in the Market

On January twenty first I had my last lesson with Lucia and said emotional goodbyes to her and to the wolf and the dingo. She gave me a coral brooch that had been in her family for two hundred years. She persisted in calling me her good luck charm; it was all quite overwhelming. Lucia had been urging me to visit Guanajuato for some time. She said it was a wonderful colonial city with a fine university - far superior to the capital in her opinion.

Later that evening there was a literary cabaret at one of the hotels given by an English group; an event sufficiently rare to ensure a packed house. All the expats were there, including a titled lady who was San Miguel's only permanent English resident, as far as I was aware. We ate chicken fajitas and drank beer into the small hours, a fitting last night for me.

I felt genuinely sad to be leaving the town; the Duke of Mantua's court had been good to me. I felt very much at home in a short space of time. Shopkeepers knew me, I had made friends and I had fallen into the lotus-eating mode. But there was the rest of Mexico to see - and Cuba. The great affair is to move, although I hate the actual business of travel, the cramped journeys on coaches, dragging my luggage around.

Full of melancholy, I indulged in some retail therapy, buying a rug as my main extravagance as well as a retablo, a holy picture painted on tin. This caught my eye because it depicted a house going up in flames with a little man wearing a sombrero and smoking a cigar. The wording explained that the cigar smoker gave thanks to the Virgin for saving his life after he had accidentally set fire to his house.

My second bag was now almost full and I spent some time packing and repacking. I booked a room at the Casa Kloster in Guanajuato, as recommended by John and made a call to my son in Los Angeles arranging for my letters to be forwarded.

Next morning I left early on the primera plus, the first class coach. This was an extravagance for me but it was a very short journey by Mexican standards, just over an hour. I was given a complimentary sandwich and a drink but the trip was mercifully too short for another bad movie to be shown. An elderly American couple came on board and told me that they were also heading for Casa Kloster.

We arrived at midday to find a city with a definite European ambience. The beautiful colonial churches were a magnificent sight, together with some fine university buildings, a museum dedicated to Cervantes and Don Quixote, and the narrowest street in the world, "the street of the kiss".

At the Casa Kloster the proprietor emerged from a large conservatory filled with palms and singing birds. He remembered John who often stayed there. The house had a large, galleried upper floor with a roof terrace and rooms opening off the gallery. I was allocated a room with a choice of three beds. The shared bathrooms were a blow, involving trips along the corridors in the small hours, but at forty pesos per night I was not going to complain.

I wandered into the centre of town and around the huge covered market before taking a bus out to see the famous momias, the mummies preserved in a Franciscan monastery.

As the bus crawled up the Carretera Panoramica to the summit of a huge hill I misheard some directions and got off too soon arriving very hot and thirsty at the museum.

The mummies have been removed from the sarcophagus of the monastery which must have been much more atmospheric. They were now in glass cases in a purpose built museum, preserved by the unique properties in their former resting place. Small, leathery cadavers with wisps of hair and shreds of clothing lay with gaping mouths in convulsive postures making one wonder uneasily about premature burial.

I felt uncomfortable with the idea that a Christian organisation would allow the dead to be exhibited in this way and even more uncomfortable that I had paid to see them. The most famous momia was the little girl aged three, buried at the beginning of the twentieth century. Perfectly preserved, she was wearing her best dress with dried flowers arranged around her. I was the last person lingering in the museum as the attendant arrived to tell me they were closing.

'Aren't you afraid?' he asked, obviously marking me down as another weird foreigner.

I managed to get back to the centre in time to visit the Cervantes museum, a lovely place and a fitting tribute to the knight of the woeful countenance. The citizens of Guanajuato obviously feel a strong affinity with Cervantes. They hold an international festival every year in his honour. Nearby was the house where the celebrated muralist Diego Rivera was born. It is now a museum.

Guanajuato means the place of the frogs in the Nahuatl language. The local parks were full of frog sculptures and frog shop signs abounded. Apparently the Nahuatl thought so little of the area that they said it was fit only for frogs. Obviously, they did not know about the silver hidden in the hills.

In the large, covered market I wandered around tasting the wares. All the markets in Mexico sell stuffed, sugar candy skulls to commemorate the day of the dead on November 1 and an astonishing selection of sweets and desserts which were originally made by nuns- Spanish sweets with a Mexican influence.

When I first visited Mexico back in the dim past of

twenty-five years ago I frequently made excuses to get away for an hour or two to visit local markets. While others wandered around ancient ruins or sipped a piña colada by the pool I spent my time looking for exotic versions of the Portobello Road. At that time the markets of Mexico were paradise for those addicted to ethnic colour and useless bargains.

In Oaxaca on my second visit I could find no trace of the donkey park where locals left their animals on market day, but a glorious rainbow of colourful textiles was displayed on various street corners.

For years I wore my woollen poncho in England when buying the cat's fish in the local open-air emporium, but there was a definite lack of exotic atmosphere in Watford. I know that the hippie peasant look has had its day, but my poncho had been hand woven by the local Indian tribe and I had purchased it after some haggling in the huge market in Toluca, a town about forty miles from Mexico City and more than eight thousand feet above sea level. I think the altitude might have induced the feeling of euphoria absent from my local High Street.

Whenever I searched for a new market experience the locals would assure me that it was "Muy tipico" and would urge me on. Where else could you find locally grown peyote (hallucinatory cactus) as well as home-made love charms, guaranteed infallible and sold by elderly ladies wearing pigtails and bowler hats? These senior citizens were full of vitality and an amazing sales patter. They usually had a steaming pot of something aromatic cooking nearby and patted out tortillas at high speed. Consequently, my kitchen became full of useless and highly ornamental souvenirs, hand-embroidered tortilla warmers and a picture of the serpent god Quetzalcoatl, for example. Anyone can have a microwave oven but few people have a genuine Aztec chocolate stirrer (machine made).

In Mexico City itself I found a market selling only toys. Stalls were piled high with marbles and dominoes. I bought a piñata there- a paper bull, frilled and pleated, ready to be stuffed with sweets on Christmas Eve. I knew it would not survive the journey home but I couldn't resist.

"Muy tipico senorita," the stallholder called after me. Every woman was called senorita, even when she had a husband and six children, it was considered complimentary. The piñata is the Mexican equivalent of the Christmas tree. It is attached to the ceiling so that the children can hit the twirling object with sticks to release the sweets and toys.

The most famous market in the capital was the Thieves' Market, held on Sunday mornings. This splendid idea should be copied everywhere. It enabled you to buy back the radio stolen from your car the week before, possibly the hub caps too.

My own excursion into this browsers' paradise was brief but dramatic. I had arrived in the plaza feeling a little under the weather. I started to walk towards the stalls when I was apparently hit over the head with a small building. When I woke up I was sitting on a chair in a nearby pharmacy with at least twenty compassionate Mexicans fanning me, waving smelling salts, patting my face and conferring about my condition. The general opinion was that I had probably drunk the water. It was well known that tourists could not drink the water. In short, I had succumbed to an attack of the aptly named Montezuma's Revenge. I was put on a course of antibiotics and boiled rice but it was at least a week before I felt human again.

Returning to Casa Kloster after my market rummage I found that the altitude had given me a headache, so after supper I opted for an early night on my creaky bed.

Next day I met some of my fellow guests; an interesting collection of travellers, students, the young, the old and the in-between. There were two English students doing courses at the university, one was a woman in her forties starting over after a divorce. A German woman had come to visit her daughter and I discovered that she worked as an au pair in Highgate, London, just around the corner from my childhood home.

A very elderly and infirm American came out of his room to announce that he had come to Casa Kloster to die. He has wintered over in Mexico for many years but this time he doesn't think that he will leave. He seemed very frail and we were all concerned because he was alone.

Down in the streets of the city I found it very difficult to orientate myself. Lucia's map was not much help. The covered alleyways or callejones must have been very picturesque in the days when lovers in capes and masks made assignations in their dark, womb-like spaces, but in modern times they have fallen prey to Mexican traffic pollution. I wondered how many people have been overcome by diesel fumes while walking through them. It was far better to wander around the plazas and narrow streets near the university eating corn-on-the-cob on a stick sold by street vendors.

The Theatre Juarez was so elegant it could have been Parisian. I was allowed in to admire the red and gold splendour of the interior, but no performances were scheduled. Swarms of students drank beer, congregated and preened themselves in the square in front of the theatre like a flock of exotic starlings.

In the evening the German lady and her daughter invited me to join them at a concert in a very modern auditorium on the outskirts of the city. We listened to Brahms and selections from Italian operas played enthusiastically, if not to the standards of London or Berlin.

The celebrated La Valenciana mine was situated a few miles outside the town. The bus deposited me in a shady square where donkeys were tied to a tree. The mine workings, the great church and the former governor's palace dominated the village but the mine did not look large by modern standards. I stood staring at the workings for a while, marvelling that most of the fabled wealth of the Spanish Empire flowed from this spot. In the late 18th century this mine was the world's largest producer of silver and it is still working today.

Guided tours of the mine were available but I declined. I have a horror of going underground. My guide book told me that the average mine worker lived for only ten years after starting his work. Not that the indigenous people, the Indios, had any choice in the matter.

The interior of the nearby church of San Cayetano was an overwhelming dazzle of gold and silver ornately carved and gilded by local Indian craftsmen in the Chirrigueresque style; an expression of the power of the Church and the wealth dug out of the ground during the colonial period. I stopped for a cool drink in a calm and lovely courtyard restaurant surrounded by Mexican antiques. Beyond the low walls I could see the tethered donkeys watching me with benevolent expressions.

The two motherly ladies who were waitresses in the café asked me where I came from. Previous experience had taught me that saying 'England' would be met with puzzled expressions. 'I'm from Europe,' I told them. When I added that I was travelling alone around Central America they looked at each other in horror and chorused, 'Pobrecita!' Poor little thing… the idea of being alone for any length of time, not to mention travelling alone, fills Mexicans with horror. For a woman it is especially tragic. The local people like to do things in groups – as large as possible. A recent pilgrimage organised in San Miguel involved several thousand people.

Kipling's belief that "*He travels fastest who travels alone,*" would not have impressed them. Of course, these rules only applied to men. Solo expeditions by either sex are a comparatively new phenomenon. In Victorian times, and almost up to the Second World War, Western rovers were accompanied by bearers, animals, guards and anyone else they could pay.

Was it my imagination or were even the donkeys giving me pitying looks? I thought of those long suffering animals as a metaphor for the indigenous people of this continent, put upon, exploited, long suffering yet resilient. They were the real reason for my travels – and to see the way the moon rose and the sun blazed over a different horizon – stronger, brighter, stranger. For these things you didn't need company.

15
A Taste for Space

Isabelle Eberhardt, the Passionate Nomad, riding around the deserts of North Africa referred to her goût d'espace, her need to get away. The modern female traveller does not have to offer elaborate excuses to justify her wanderings. A desire to see the world, or just for the hell of it, are reasons usually accepted by everyone. Victorian travellers, dromomaniacs and drapetomaniacs all, had to give more specific reasons. Women did not just take off in those days; only men could claim that activity as a basic right.

Some of the reasons dreamed up by the early women travellers were eccentric at best and sometimes pointless, to say the least. Margaret Fountaine's excuse for a lifetime's wandering around the globe was to collect butterflies. After years of decimating nature she bequeathed her collection to a museum in Suffolk, but her two volumes of racy reminiscences are what people remember.

Mary Kingsley, the awesomely intrepid woman who set out for West Africa, the white man's grave, because she had a spare six months had never been abroad apart from one week's stay in Paris and a short trip to the Canary Islands. Her intention was to collect specimens of fresh water fish. In the teeth of this unlikely excuse she became a respected ethnologist and naturalist despite having had no formal education.

Her real reason for swapping her monotonous existence as family housekeeper for the thrills and rigours of West Africa might have been to exact a kind of revenge on her father. George Kingsley had been a globetrotting physician and naturalist who wrote exciting letters home to his family describing his adventures. He did not think it worthwhile to spend money on his daughter's education; she was to be the unpaid family housekeeper, nothing more.

After her parents' death Mary broke away with a vengeance. She went from Victorian domesticity to West Africa in one leap; a dramatic exodus to find some meaning in her dreadfully proscribed life. She told acquaintances nonchalantly that she was going to die in Africa because the world had no further use for her. Happily, she survived for many more years.

She vindicated herself by discovering several new species and being the first white person to cross the rainforests from the Ogowe River to the Rembwe, although she was never given credit for this by the Royal Geographical Society.

Travellers today are a sad crew in comparison. With no new territories to discover, no terrible conditions to endure, our journeys have become interior ones. Our sufferings are the ones involved in spending a night sleeping at the airport because a flight has been cancelled. When Mary reached the Gold Coast she was shown two freshly dug graves and told, "We always keep these ready for Europeans." There were no vaccinations for deadly diseases. Today we are given solemn warnings on how to avoid prickly heat rash.

I was thinking about the perils of travel when I made the short but eventful trip from Merida in Mexico to Cuba on one of Cubana Airlines elderly prop aircraft. After my adventures at the airport when I opted out of carrying a parcel to Havana for a distraught Yorkshireman, the only thing I had to worry about was the unpressurised cabin that caused painful ear popping.

On the return journey I was blissfully unaware that an aerial dogfight was taking place nearby between Cuban and American planes. We narrowly escaped being another statistic in that long-running affair but somehow it didn't compare with Mary Kingsley's laconic entries in her journal describing the difficulty of preventing her servants from being eaten by the local tribe of cannibals who were offering hospitality.

She would have ignored the warnings given to me in Mexico about travelling at night. Everyone repeated *never travel at night* like a mantra. The country's numerous brigands do a lot of business after sundown, even waylaying coaches occasionally.

I remembered this as I departed on the overnight coach for Graham Greene country; that area of southern Mexico described in *The Lawless Roads* as one of his least favourite places. Vilahermosa was to be the stopover at three in the morning.

It is difficult to form an impression of a place seen only as a nondescript bus station in the middle of the night. A blurred image of featureless suburban roads was all I could absorb - nothing that justified its beautiful town tag.

Greene said that the men of this place were notoriously aggressive due to eating too much iguana meat. The only natives I saw were dispirited bus drivers propped against a wall as they smoked a cigarette between shifts.

A quartet of English students doing the Grand Tour, now known as the gap year, were on the coach. The only time I came across so many fellow countrymen and women in one place. It was not an exciting encounter: these young people were as stand-offish and supercilious as their colonial great grandparents would have been, disdaining the locals and my small, dishevelled self as not worthy of their attention.

Margaret Fountaine also had the Victorian Englishwoman's tendency to despise the locals. She reminisced while en route to Australia in 1914-

I remember when I was quite a small child I told my mother one day: 'Mamma, when I grow up I mean to be a loose adventurer,' and I could not imagine why my mother rather reproved me for the remark. My idea of being a 'loose adventurer' having been to go to Australia and break in wild horses.

And now I was in Australia, the land of my childish dreams, but how different was I finding it. We did not care much for the passengers on this boat, and indeed we had already begun to experience that nearly all the Australians are commonplace in the extreme, especially the women and girls.

Maria Caroline Bolitho was another globe trotter who left candid portraits of the people and places she visited. Her journals are largely unknown but their keen observations and lively style deserve a wider audience. This Cornishwoman from a distinguished family of bankers was one of the first female members of the Royal Geographical Society.

In 1896 she set out with a friend for Ladakh on the border with Tibet. They visited remote monasteries and witnessed the devil dances at Hemis which had seldom been seen by Europeans. They returned to Simla over passes at 17,000-18,000 feet at the wrong time of year, digging ponies out of snow drifts and urging on the unwilling native bearers who knew only too well how dangerous the situation was.

Maria Caroline was unfazed; she was not affected by altitude sickness and took cold, hardship and terrible food in her stride. She was equally confident when visiting the ruby mines of Burma, travelling over roads infested by dacoits or being insulted by Chinese during the Boxer rebellion. Leaving her companion behind, she travelled solo in Sikkim reaching the border of Tibet which was then closed to foreigners.

In Ladakh she began her crossing of the notorious Baralacha pass, *"despite great reluctance being shown."*

The Pass and the whole range of the Baralacha were entirely hidden by the clouds that were hung so low that we could only see a few yards in front of us. The snow which at starting was only to the depth of two feet became deeper and deeper, until in some places it rose to the girths.... Later another hazard appeared.

There was a crashing sound and I saw to my horror that two large stones were bounding down the mountain side and that it was impossible for us to pass before they fell. It was a case of whoever lost their presence of mind would be killed.

Naturally, Maria Caroline did not lose anything. Her recollections were of darkness, snow and whizzing stones. Undeterred she rode on, accompanied by yaks and nomads and the long suffering companion referred to only as *"The other memsahib."* She commented that the Ladakhis were squat and unattractive but honest and sunny natured, unlike the grasping, dishonest Kashmiris.

When Victorian female travellers were set on reaching a place, nothing could stand in their way. In 1813, Lady Hester Stanhope decided to see Palmyra despite being advised against it. She set off by herself with a few Arab companions.

I was treated with the greatest respect and hospitality, and it was the most curious sight I ever saw; horses and mares fed upon camels' milk; Arabs living on little except rice; the space around me covered with living things; 1600 camels coming to water from one tribe only; the old poets from the banks of the Euphrates singing the praises of the ancient heroes; women with lips dyed bright blue and nails red, and hands all over flowers and different designs; a chief who is obeyed like a great king; starvation and pride so mixed that really I could not have had an idea of it... However, I have every reason to be perfectly content with their conduct towards me, and I am the Queen with them all...

It is difficult for women today to appreciate how heady and liberating this life must have been for the few women who were able to break away from ordinary life in Europe. Hester embraced her new life, praising everything and belittling everything English. She met Lord Byron but thought little of him. He was not good looking in her opinion, having a look of depravity. As for his poetry...*It is easy enough to write verses!*

After half an hour we climbed back into the coach and I tried to sleep as the vehicle sped towards the state of Chiapas and the driver's radio blared out salsa rhythms. I was intrigued by the Mexican way of coping with long distance driving. The coach carried a relief driver who slept on a mattress inside the luggage hold. I wondered how they managed to avoid suffocation.

Coach travel has always had its disadvantages, even for the wife of an ambassador. When the resolute Scotswoman, Frances Inglis (Madame Calderon de la Barca) was forced to travel by public coach in Mexico in the 1840s she coped by invoking the Stiff Upper Lip.

We climbed into the coach, which was so crowded that we could but just turn our heads to groan an adieu to our friends. The coach rattled off through the streets, dashed through the Alameda, and gradually we began to shake down and, by a little arrangement of cloaks and sarapes, to be less crowded. A padre with a very Indian complexion sat between K---and me, and a horrible, long, lean, bird-like female with immense red goggle-eyes, coal-black teeth, fingers like claws, a great goitre, and drinking brandy at intervals, sat opposite to us. There were also various men buried in their sarapes. Satisfied with a cursory inspection of our companions, I addressed myself to Blackwood's magazine....

I addressed myself to the Guide to Central America before dozing off.

16
Oaxaca-Vera Cruz
"Like fabrics of enchantment piled to heaven"
(Percy Bysshe Shelley)

After leaving Guanajuato I returned briefly to Mexico City to change direction towards the State of Oaxaca. I hoped this would be an opportunity to see the real Mexico, less tourist-ridden and with fewer resident gringos. Travelling south from the capital the city of Oaxaca was five hundred and thirty kilometres away.

When I arrived in the Zocolo, the main square in Oaxaca, the combined crowds, noise, heat and dust created cultural overload in an exhilarating way. It was already dusk and a festival was in full swing. Indian rain dances were being performed by dancers in multi-hued feathers and extravagant costumes.

When I had orientated myself I gradually learnt the names of the best budget cafés and dimly lit grocery stores tucked away in side streets. Back at the pension where I had booked a room I found another vast, empty old house where the water was seldom on and there was no overhead fan. I lay in bed admiring the high-ceilinged room with its solid Victorian hotel attributes, the marble floor and the tall, graceful windows.

The street outside was quiet and the café next door where I had breakfast soon became a second home. The proprietor's wife nodded and smiled at me as she chopped small, green bananas for frying. Strangely named Oaxacan dishes were on the menu which she was unable to describe to me. I suspected that her Spanish was as unreliable as mine. Many of the local people spoke only their own language.

Oaxaca was a stronghold of the Zapotec people and beyond the city lay the huge and incredible remains of their city, Monte Alban. The vast treasure of gold taken from the ancient site can be seen in the city museum and little remains of a once great civilisation from two thousand and five hundred years ago; a people who believed that their works would last forever. The Zapotec and Mixtec peoples invented writing in Mexico, a form of hieroglyphics, as well as the famous astrological calendar reproduced today on everything from tea towels to silver rings.

These people excelled in astronomy, made fine ceramic work and magnificent gold jewellery. Craftsmen in the city still make covetable reproductions of the designs from the Monte Alban treasure.

Nothing now remains of their sophisticated political and social structure and elaborate religious rituals, just this immense, overgrown ruin with vast dusty plazas, an observatory oriented towards magnetic south, stone friezes showing enemies being castrated and empty ball courts where the losers paid with their lives in ritualistic games. The entire Zapotec culture is an enigma, their hieroglyphics still undeciphered. Anthroplogists can only speculate on how they lived their lives, how they governed themselves and what their beliefs were.

Today, their copper-skinned descendants conduct their lives in a way that involves passing through the main square at least twice a day - to keep in touch. Wandering through the square in the velvety darkness I wondered how the English managed to keep a community together without a Zocolo. We have only the supermarket as a substitute.

Throngs of people were passing up and down the cathedral steps while others sat on the steps lighting candles.

I struggled to recall which feast day was being celebrated, but in Mexico pre-Christian ceremonies merge seamlessly with the feasts of the church. I ate a mango ice-cream as I watched the celebrations. The colour and ritual in daily life here was almost overwhelming but also addictive and exciting especially when contrasted with the general drabness of every day life in Britain.

The dancers and singers were still performing and small children were letting off fire-crackers. Vendors of sweets and balloons were everywhere and on the sidelines weary salespeople rested on park benches. In repose, the faces of Mexican people told their own story. Melancholy was written large on their dark features and reality poked through the merry-making. Perhaps the lights and fireworks, the songs and dances served now, as in the past, to placate the harsh gods of this land.

That morning in the café where I ate breakfast, I met an Englishman, an event unusual enough to be written in exclamation marks in my journal. In a country overrun with North Americans the British are rarely encountered. This was one of its charms for me. I have met this man before; he was my companion on the long coach trip from Mexico City, the one I christened the melancholy civil servant. He had told me about his extended two years' leave of absence from a government department, mainly spent travelling in Latin America. I had not realised that the civil service was such an obliging employer.

The melancholy one spoke excellent Spanish and had an empathy with the land and the people. I wondered if he would ever return to his dull desk job and his house in Brighton. The travelling life is an addictive one. The lure of the next horizon is like a siren song. The past and our present problems fade away and there is only the here and now. Already, my former life in England seemed very remote and unreal.

Rob and I ate breakfast together while he philosophised. He wished me good luck and goodbye before setting off for the bus station. He tried to persuade me to change my itinerary and visit the bays of Huatulco 'Before it's too late.' I remembered that this was the spectacularly beautiful area on the coast of Oaxaca that was scheduled to be turned into the next Cancun by the Mexican government. I regretted that I wouldn't get to see them. I was committed to going on to Vera Cruz, jumping around the country like a Mexican jumping bean.

I stayed in the city for a while, exploring colonial churches and seeking out little cafés where people went to drink mescal, the local spirit, as well as tequila. In the Café Hipotesis you could drink the quirkily named 'thoughtful' tequila while admiring the books on philosophy that lined the walls.

I discovered that I could enjoy one of my favourite childhood puddings with an exotic Oaxacan twist – chocolate bread pudding with cactus fruit sauce. My grandfather always made our family puddings and I wondered what he would have thought of the Mexican version.

Once, I peered through the gate into an exquisite garden in a former convent, now an expensive hotel for visiting North Americans. It was a world away from my hot, airless pension. Every morning I would complain bitterly about the lack of hot water -or any other kind. The concierge would shrug and say that I was not manipulating the taps correctly. Perhaps I was supposed to chant an ancient Zapotecan incantation as well, but I never found out. I tried to persuade him to come up to the room to investigate but he said he could not be bothered. It was too hot to make an issue of it so I went next door for a cold drink.

Later I went in search of a place that would mend my broken reading glasses. An arm had snapped off and I had forgotten to bring a spare pair. In a back street I found a small optometrist's shop where the assistant spent a long time searching through boxes until he found a virtually identical arm. He fixed it on and refused cash saying that he was glad to be of service. I insisted on leaving a small payment. Recycling is a way of life here, not a fashionable alternative. Back home I would have been obliged to buy a new pair.

Before I left the city I tried to reconfirm my flight home from LA to London, only to discover that the airline had no record of my booking. It says much for my state of mind that my reaction was one of pleasure. Now I would have to stay in Mexico!

I returned to the Zocolo and sat drinking in the colour and sounds once more; willing myself to remember everything. Would I ever come this way again? Female travellers in the past also promised themselves that they would remember their special places forever. Amelia Edwards writing in the quiet of suburban Bristol recorded in A *Thousand Miles up the Nile;*

"I look; I listen; I promise myself that I will remember it all in years to come- all the solemn hills, these silent colonnades, these deep, quiet places of shadow, these sleeping palms."

Before leaving the city I re-established my flight home with some reluctance before planning the next long coach trip.

The four hour coach journey across country to Vera Cruz was enlivened by a particularly violent film about the IRA, watched avidly by the other passengers. I tried to sleep or read but the noise level was too high. Outside, a hurricane was blowing itself out. The palm trees waved almost to the ground in the wind and fat, tropical raindrops fell amid the steaming vegetation. The bus edged along perilous ravines with a sheer drop inches away from unreliable tyres. Hair raising bus journeys have always been a feature of travel in

Latin America. I coped by closing my eyes and praying furiously to a variety of gods.

When Marianne North was in similar situations she coped by shouting at the natives or just sitting out the situation. Marooned in a closed carriage called a gharry while en route to Darjeeling, she found that the road had been almost washed way. At dawn the road was only a few inches above water.

I arrived with a pounding headache caused either by the IRA or the grey, sultry hurricane weather, but I found Vera Cruz to be my kind of place. The Hotel Amparo, recommended in the guide book, was warm and comfortable and only forty pesos per night. I swallowed an aspirin and went in search of food.

The central square, the Plaza Constitución was white, colonial in style and filled with cafés, flowers and marimba bands. I ate a huge bowl of fresh tropical fruits and coconut before exploring the town. Enormous oil tankers were moored in the bay and souvenir stalls lined the Malécon, the harbourside boulevard. It felt good to be on the Caribbean coast again.

In the evening, after a short siesta, I watched couples dancing to the marimbas and wished for once that I had a companion. No situation is perfect, as those Victorian travellers discovered. A companion can be a nuisance. He travels fastest who travels alone – and so does she.

One of the dancers caught my attention. He was dressed in a white suit with his bottom stuck out at a jaunty angle, his ponytail flying as he swung his partner. The local dances were the bamba and the zapateado in the Jarocho style. These owe something to Spanish flamenco with much stamping and hand clapping. Harps and guitars were part of the accompaniment.

The next day was a public holiday with the weather still damp and sultry as I made my way to the bus station to buy a ticket for Catemaco tomorrow. My route lay through the market where I bought a jar of concha cream, allegedly made from conch shells and guaranteed to transform the complexion.

I had bought a miracle cream in Romania and now I was doing the same thing again. Travel always leaves you open to possibilities. I suspect it was always so. Lady Mary Wortley Montagu in Turkey was less than enthusiastic about a cream called Balm of Mecca. News of this wonder had reached her friends at home.

As to the Balm of Mecca, I will certainly send you some, but it is not as easily got as you suppose and I cannot in conscience advise you to make use of it. I know not how it comes to have such universal applause. All the ladies of my acquaintance in London and Vienna have begged me to send pots of it to them. I have had a present of a small quantity (which I assure you is very valuable) of the best sort, and with great joy I applied it to my face, expecting some wonderful effect to my advantage. The next morning the change indeed was wonderful; my face was swelled to a very extraordinary size and all over red...it remained in this lamentable state for three days, during which you may be sure I passed my time very ill.

I noticed very little change after using the concha cream; I decided that my clear complexion must be due to plenty of fresh air and exercise. Lady Mary wrote,
Let my complexion take its natural course and decay in its own due time. That was my philosophy too, although, in Lady Mary's case it must have been disappointing. Her former good looks had been ruined by smallpox.

Out on the Malécon a couple were washing cars and having a matrimonial fight. He looked shifty and sullen while his distraught partner abused him for his infidelity. The man shrugged and wandered off as she screamed curses at his back and then sobbed against one of the wet cars.

Nothing was open on this holiday and so I boarded a boat for a gusty trip across the bay to the old Spanish fort. A middle aged couple started a conversation with me. They had lived in Vera Cruz for thirty years and loved the place. He was a New Yorker and she was from Madrid. Their friends, a visiting French couple, nodded their heads in agreement, saying how much they liked the town.

They recommended a local fish restaurant for my lunch, big, busy place where I was the only foreigner – always a good sign. I enjoyed sea bass stuffed with shrimps at a bargain price. When I ordered a beer the waiter solemnly assured me that no alcohol could be served on national holidays.

On the way back to the hotel I watched a procession of local people carrying Communist flags calling for better conditions for the workers. Rifle-toting guards stood in shop doorways as they passed. Intimidation is the name of the political game here.

Next day I took a short bus ride to Catemaco, a small town on the shores of a huge and beautiful volcanic lake. Fishing boats lined the pebbled shores and silver and purple mountains framed the cobalt blue water. The town has two claims to fame, first as a popular weekend retreat for the people of Vera Cruz and, from way back, as the home of the largest collection of witches and warlocks in the country - occult central, in fact. I first heard about Catemaco while I was visiting a museum of folk lore and, naturally I had to visit the place.

When I arrived and wandered through the streets the town seemed to be almost deserted. It was an off-season weekday and most of the restaurants and bars were closed. I checked into another empty hotel overlooking the lake. The proprietor gave me a room key, took my money and vanished. I never saw him again – or any other member of staff. I was the only guest.

I ate the small, tasty flat fish from the lake in an empty, open-air café and then sat on the harbour wall writing up my notes to the amusement of passers by. The merriment and incredulity shown towards women travelling alone, especially older women, is only exceeded by the reaction to a lone female traveller with a notebook. The stout-hearted Mary Kingsley had this problem in West Africa, in pidgin English-

"Where be your husband, ma?"

"I no got one."

"No got one, ma?"

"No," I said furiously, *"Do you get much rubber around here?"*

An elderly man stopped to chat with me for a while. He was dignified and friendly but eventually he asked me for money. The function of the foreign traveller in this country is to be the eternally rich outsider. I wished I could stay long enough to attempt some kind of integration.

Later I spoke to a fisherman who was smoking a cigarette on the beach. Trying to sound casual I asked about the witches and warlocks. Were there many around? He assured me matter-of-factly that there were still quite a few in the town.

'Can I meet one?' He promised to arrange it and next morning when I emerged from the hotel I found a shifty looking character waiting to lead me to the bruja (witch) who will predict my future.

'We must go to her house now,' he urged me as we rushed along a side street. He looked anxiously over his shoulder and I suspected that the local Tourist Bureau had banned this particular form of free enterprise. My guide quoted a price of seventy pesos and I agreed as he almost pushed me through the door of a small, typical Mexican villa. He rushed off at remarkable for speed for someone dragging a lame leg.

The bruja looked like any modern Mexican woman, well dressed with a fashionable hairdo. She told me that she came from a long line of sorcerers and her assistant nodded in agreement. The assistant was a younger woman who sat at the table with us but said nothing. I decided she was either the daughter, a bodyguard or the sorcerer's apprentice.

Although they seemed normal enough they both had a faint air of menace that matched the atmosphere of the town with its brooding volcanoes at the end of the street. This was definitely Malcolm Lowry country.

I decided not to give much information to the witch. She would have to work for her money. I told her only the obvious facts; I was from England, a foreigner travelling alone. Leaning back in her chair the bruja proceeded to give me a terrifyingly accurate précis of my past life and recent events. I was so shocked I could only sit rigidly in my chair while she told me that I had no home (I had sold my house), I had recently suffered a death in the family (my father), I had severe money problems(!) I had lost my way in life.

Of course, some of this could have been good guesswork but to know all of it seemed extraordinary. As I listened I felt my usual scepticism draining away and my skin crawling a little. At the end of her speech she asked me if her analysis had been correct. When I gasped 'Yes,' her assistant smiled knowingly.

I came sharply back to reality as the bruja told me that my stars needed cleansing to rid me of the bad luck and bad vibes around me. She was willing to conduct a ceremony of "cleansing fire" at a cost of $25. My tight budget would not allow for luxuries like this. I realized that everyone was given a bad message and the same sales pitch but I was still stunned by the accuracy of the reading. When I declined her offer both women looked furious. I wondered uneasily about Aztec human sacrifices and wondered whether I would get out of the house in one piece.

I hurriedly put the money on the table and started backing towards the door. The bruja told me I was being very foolish but otherwise made no attempt to stop me. Her apprentice just glared. I would love to have had the ceremony of cleansing fire out of anthropological interest and in the cause of good copy, but twenty five dollars represented a couple of nights lodging on my anaemic budget.

As I stumbled into the street the shifty looking man sidled up asking for a tip. I gave him some loose change which he spat on saying it was only enough for a refresco, a soft drink. He muttered something about dollars and tequila before walking off with that curious, shambling gait, the result of having one leg shorter than the other. Now two people would probably call down curses on my head.

Anyone who believed in this sort of thing would have realized that I had wasted my money being told things I already knew. The whole point would have been to have the cleansing ceremony, but the point for me was simply curiousity. Like Mary Kingsley, I was fascinated by ethnology. I had read Fraser's *Golden Bough* and Lévi-Strauss and I also had a pre-occupation with ritual and fetish and the myth of vampirism in particular. This might have been the result of growing up near the crumbling ruins of Highgate cemetery, or simply reading unsuitable books at an early age.

I was sure that the ceremony would have involved donating some of my hair, nail clippings or blood. The belief in the ability to obtain power over people by these means is a universal one, from Devon to the Mississippi, from West Africa to Latin America.

Mary Kingsley described how the first white settlers in West Africa were forever vomiting because the local cooks were putting unpalatable charms in the food to gain power over their masters.

I regretted my decision but consoled myself with a trip on the lake with some of the fishermen. I left flowers at the shrine of the Virgin of Catemaco, patron of the fisher folk, with only the men and a flock of seabirds looking on. The colour of the water, almost violet with a creamy foam, was magical and unlike anything I had ever seen; different from the azure of the Mediterranean, the green of the Caribbean or the wine-dark sea of the Greeks.

The next morning, Sunday, I was in Catemaco's tiny bus station writing a letter to Lucia in San Miguel and waiting for the bus back to Vera Cruz. It was only eight thirty and the place was empty apart from myself and a little old lady with a large bundle. I couldn't shake off the feeling of unease I had felt since I arrived. The almost empty town seemed cowed by the volcanoes breathing down its neck. If a town could be described as neurotic then Catemaco had definite Freudian tendencies. Perhaps the witches were there to provide the therapy. I had decided to do what the practical Mary Kingsley always did when anything unpleasant happened on her travels. I was legging it as fast as possible in the other direction.

If I had come when the holiday makers were around the atmosphere might have been different but I was not convinced. Graham Greene often remarked on the brooding atmosphere of Mexican towns. If he had noticed then that was good enough for me. Sentences about witchcraft in Dahomey from Mary Kingsley's book came into my head-

"Why has this man not been buried?"

"It is fetish that has killed him and he must lie here exposed with nothing on him until only the bones remain," is the cheerful answer. This sounded discouraging to a person whose occupation would necessitate going about considerably in boats and whose fixed desire was to study fetish."

I sympathized; I was glad to be back in carefree Vera Cruz with time for another wonderful fruit salad before leaving on another coach journey to the northern part of the state.

I had a special reason for wanting to visit Papantla in northern Veracruz State. The town was the centre of one of the largest vanilla producing regions in the world and the heady scent of the vanilla orchid lies over the area. After my first visit to Mexico many years ago I had written a novel called after the orchid goddess and set in Mexico. I had never actually visited the place and I had not seen the voladores, the flying Totonac Indians.

On certain feast days a thirty-foot pole with a rotating platform on the top is erected and four voladores (flyers) attach themselves to the column with ropes and spin around the structure, making a flying descent. A musician remains on the platform playing a pipe and drum. The ceremony is dedicated to the rain god and it takes place at the pyramid of El Tajin about twelve kilometres outside Papantla.

We drove through orchid forests as the vegetation grew greener and lusher by the minute. It was still rainy and chilly after the recent hurricane and I wished I had some warmer clothing.

I arrived in the town during the afternoon on February 2nd, Candlemas day. People were making their way to the various churches carrying their candles, passing a giant mural of the voladores adorning the main square. The inscription proclaimed *Homenaje a la Cultura Totonac*.

I checked into a miserable, unheated, low budget room nearby and persuaded the reluctant receptionist to bring me an extra blanket. My bed had only one thin cover and the whole place felt damp.

My first priority was a very late lunch and I ate a good fish meal in a local café before heading to the market, the Mercado Hidalgo. Among the poultry and vegetables were stalls selling textiles and various objects made from the vanilla bean pod, small animals, baskets and scented vanilla sachets. There was also a liqueur called cream of vanilla that tasted foul. Fortunately, I love the smell, if not the taste.

Papantla was not as perfumed and picturesque as I had imagined but I think it was the real Mexico - Graham Greene country. The rain was growing heavier and I was forced to buy an umbrella, not an item usually associated with this place.

There was a small tourist office nearby, big enough for one official who seemed genuinely surprised to see a tourist, especially at this time of year. She explained where to find the bus that would take me to El Tajin in the morning. It was a magnificent sight, she assured me, and the voladores would fly. There was a new museum at the site but I was warned to watch out for chiggers as I walked around. These nasty little creatures hide in the grass until they can attach themselves to you and burrow into your skin. Thus reassured I went back to read my guidebook and then to watch the Candlemas service at the cathedral.

After an uncomfortable and sleepless night due to the cold I envied Alexandra David-Néel, the first western woman to reach the forbidden city of Lhasa. She became a Buddhist and perfected the art of thumo reskiang, raising the body's temperature through meditation. Of course, it had taken her three years to acquire this ability and I couldn't spare the time. David-Néel was made of stern stuff, capable of walking for nineteen hours in the Himalayan foothills without a break and claiming not to feel tired – only sleepy.

I tried to while away the sleepless hours by thinking about my relative comfort compared with my Victorian predecessors. There was corseted Mary Kingsley ignoring bodily ills and Kate Marsden whose contribution to travel literature was the wonderfully titled *On Sledge and Horseback to Outcast Siberian Lepers.* With total English ignorance of foreign parts (still observable today), she arrived in Moscow in a light woollen coat with a large supply of plum puddings donated by a friend.

In darkest Siberia she faced a trek across frozen wastes with remarkable aplomb, surviving on appalling food, buoyed up by her vision of helping the abandoned lepers of the Russian Empire. By this time she had donned more appropriate clothing. Layered in furs and wool…*I am afraid I used to feel rather a cruel satisfaction when I lay down at night and realized that I was probably crushing with my body weight a good many of the black beetles that would otherwise have crawled over me while I slept.*

She wisely made it a rule never to watch how her food was prepared. Her diet was mainly black bread, tea and occasionally a wild duck, supplemented by the plum puddings.

Kate received little acknowledgement from the Establishment for her heroic journey and the improvements she made to the lives of the lepers. Queen Victoria, however, admired her and sent her a jewelled brooch. The Russian Empress sent letters and thanks. I couldn't see any black beetles in my damp room, but I didn't look too hard.

Next morning I boarded the bus thinking that I would be the only gringa on board. My fellow passengers were all Totonacs, a few of them still wearing the traditional costume, baggy white trousers and sailor-style shirts for the men, lacy skirts and embroidered shawls for the women.

A small boy accompanying his grandparents wore a batman outfit under his serape. I was saddened to see that the dignified, grey haired woman sitting next to me was barefoot. There is so much unnecessary poverty in Mexico, one of the world's largest oil producers.

Madame Calderon de la Barca endured a few uncomfortable journeys during her Mexican sojourn. I think she would have recognised many of my fellow travellers.

Occasionally, she enjoyed the equivalent of a trip on a primera plus coach. On one occasion she was invited into a flamboyant carriage that had once belonged to the French king. After the fall of the régime the coach was bought and sold and eventually sent to Mexico.

A most luxurious travelling coach, entirely covered with gilding, save where the lilies of France surmount the crown...lined with white satin with violet-coloured binding. In former days, from its gilded and showy appearance, it would have brought any price; but the taste for gaudy equipages has gone by since the introduction of foreign, and especially of English carriages; and the present proprietor, who bought it for its intrinsic good qualities, paid but a moderate sum for it. In this carriage, drawn by six strong horses, with two first-rate coachmen and several outriders well-armed, we went along at great speed. The drivers, dressed Mexican fashion, with all their accoutrements smart and new, looked very picturesque. Jackets and trousers of deerskin, and jackets embroidered in green, with hanging silver buttons, the trousers also embroidered and slit up the side of the leg, trimmed with silver buttons and showing an underpair of bleached linen; these, with the postillions' boots, and great hats with gold rolls, form a dress which would faire fureur, if some adventurous Mexican would venture to display it on the streets of London.

When we stopped on the edge of Papantla I was surprised to see another Western woman get on the bus. We hailed each other like Stanley and Livingstone. I went to sit with her and she introduced herself as a young French-Canadian student spending a year at the university in Mexico City. She was researching slang, graffiti and scatological language for her thesis; apparently the Totonacs were noted for these. Much of the research involved reading the walls in men's toilets.

I marvelled at how things had changed since my own

college days. Veronique was fluent in several languages and agreed to spend the day with me at El Tajin. She was keen to see the voladores and I was able to tell her about the vanilla goddess.

El Tajin means hurricane and the site contains the ruins of what was the Totonac capital. Among the monuments is the amazing pyramid of the niches with three hundred and sixty five openings like a beehive. We walked around the huge site while the guide warned us about snakes and a large, malevolent, poisonous centipede that attacks your legs. At that moment the pouring rain and cold seemed more threatening. We could not get warm despite several coffees.

The museum was well stocked with Totonac artefacts but the figure that excited me the most was outside on a souvenir stall. There she was, Xanath, the vanilla goddess herself. She was depicted kneeling down; a large breasted, naked fertility figure wearing what looked like a huge feathered headdress. Her face was grotesque to Western eyes, the ugliest and meanest face I had seen on any Aztec, Totonac, Olmec or any other Mexican god. Somehow, I was not disappointed; she exuded energy and vitality, something both sinister and erotic. Veronique was puzzled by my pre-occupation with her. She tugged at my arm, saying that the voladores were about to fly.

We watched, fascinated, as the five men began their ascent of the pole. The musician perched on the top and began to beat his drum as the others attached themselves to their ropes. As graceful as swallows they plunged from the top head downwards and began to fly around the pole. The piping and drumming grew louder and more urgent as the men drew closer to the ground. They wore vivid red, blue and fuschia pink trousers, embroidered serapes and headbands and white shirts. The musician had a jaunty yellow cockade in his hat.

If there are enough tourists around the flyers perform every day. Formerly they flew only on important feast days such as Corpus Christi. The ancient religious rites have blended seamlessly into the calendar of the Christian church and the ritual had certainly proved effective. The rain had grown heavier all the time, stopping only while the voladores performed.

Veronique and I sat under an awning and ordered some warming chicken soup. She told me about the Chichimeca people. The name means "sons of bitches." It sounded as if studying scatological language was a lot of fun. Later, she was taking a bus back to Poza Rico where she was staying with a friend and I had one more night in the cheerless pension before heading back to Vera Cruz City.

I managed to beg yet another thin cover for my bed and as I lay there feeling sorry for myself I remembered the wonderfully focused and determined Cornish lady, Maria Caroline Bolitho sleeping on bare floors in unheated Himalayan houses with only her pith helmet for a pillow and an English raincoat for a cover.

17
Merida –Small Mahogany Men Wielding Machetes

My memories of the little capital of the Yucatan, tempered by an overnight coach journey with freezing air conditioning, were of a small, tropical, cheerful, laid back place. I came and went at various times and my base was the Hotel Trinidad, a place similar to Casa Kloster in Guanajuato, and as empty as La Huerta in San Miguel.

I found a nearby laundry where I handed over my few threads to the usual obliging ladies before falling asleep in my room to a background of cats singing, music playing and sirens wailing faintly in the distance. Everyone was gearing up for Carnival which was a week away.

Merida's zócalo was small but completely in the Spanish colonial style: white and candy pink palaces and churches flanked the small, central garden. The former governor's palace contained wonderful portraits and tile work; horse drawn carriages waited outside the building.

The town was full of visitors fleeing the northern winter; cafés overflowed with Americans, Canadians and even the occasional Brit. In a travel agency near the hotel the French-Canadian proprietor told me that he could arrange my trip to Cuba 'At rock-bottom prices,' flying on Cubana Airlines, Aeroflot's little sister.

On February 10th I took a bus out to Progreso, a small, unassuming, slightly scruffy seaside town near Merida. The beach at Chexalub was deserted and I sat in the sun with a bit of an El Norte blowing to cool things down. A number of elderly Americans spend the winter here and many of the beach-front houses were owned by people from Mexico City. These were deserted at this time of year and often available for rent at reasonable prices.

I chatted to people in cafés where I ate fresh fish for lunch. Progreso was like a smaller, tattier version of Vera Cruz; people were always happy to give you directions to the post office, although they couldn't tell you when it might be open. An expressive shrug usually meant after the post master's siesta. Later, I took a collective taxi back to Merida where groups were dancing in the streets, rehearsing for carnival.

On Sunday I queued for a free ticket to see the folkdance and song show at the beautiful University theatre. This was another Spanish colonial gem in pink, white and gold - or perhaps it was a more recent copy. Two Americans from Oregon stood with me but I found a seat next to a friendly, motherly local woman who worked at the casa de cultura. She handed me a hand painted invitation card saying,

'If you are travelling alone, come to see the crowning of the junior carnival queen on Wednesday.' Then, with a riot of colour, stamping and hooting, the performance began.

The music was Spanish influenced crossed with the lively folk dances of Mexico. The costumes blended the vivid colours of the ancient native peoples with the styles of the European grandees of a past century. The dancers were a whirl of white lace and black velvet with colourful satin shirts - and that was just the men.

Afterwards, when I went in search of my comida I asked for pork but was given chicken as usual. This always happened to me in Mexico. I was never sure whether my Spanish was at fault or if they were out of pork and didn't like to mention the fact.

I managed to track down two dog-eared English paperbacks at the hotel left by former guests. The book situation was dire.

The carnival preparations made me feel quite left out of things, so I arranged to visit the famed ruins at Chichen-Itza on the hottest day so far. The heat at the pyramids was quite pole-axing and it was only February. Together with Teotithuacan in Mexico City, these are the most visited relics of Pre-Columbian Mexico. I wished the tourists and souvenir sellers were a million miles away. It must be wonderful to visit the more remote ruins in the jungle where coach trippers were absent.

In the shattering heat I gazed up at the pyramid called El Castillo and the carved images of the plumed serpent god Kukulkan. I had read the Mayan prophecy which states that Kukulkan will rise from beneath the playing field at Chichen Itza on December 22nd 2012 and bring about the end of the world.

For the peoples of Meso- America time was inextricably bound up with religion. The various highly complex calendars developed by the Maya were far more accurate than our own – only one day off out of six thousand years. Perhaps their prophecy will come true. The end of the world has been a constant pre-occupation of mankind, with the emphasis on man.

The Maya believed that the world had ended and been reborn several times. What a fascinating and mysterious puzzle the ancient peoples of Latin America present to the world; such complex civilisations which had never managed to invent the wheel.

Their beliefs are so far removed from our own – their obsession with human sacrifice and their Janus-like, reptilian gods. Today, largely stripped of their ancient faith, the Mayan people retain many cultural quirks from the past. Their idea of beauty is very different from our own. They still favour the cross-eyed look and long, backward sloping foreheads. One of their few benevolent beliefs was that women who died in childbirth automatically went to heaven.

After an inspection of the playing field and ball court where the ritual games were held I collapsed under a tree for some meagre shade as sweat poured down my face. A nearby vendor waved an image of the serpent god over my head. It was tastefully woven on a terracotta coloured cloth.

I met an English girl near the great pyramid and we arranged to eat lunch together in Merida. She was planning to take a job in Brussels after her trip, confessing that she was travelling to get over an unhappy love affair. So many people travel for the wrong reasons; travelling is an end in itself.

The extraordinary nomad, Isabelle Eberhardt, ranging far and wide with only her horse and dog for company had grown up in the prim suburbs of Geneva and longed to get away, to feel the desert sand underfoot and the desert winds in her face.

For the British, squeezed on her majesty's tiny, dysfunctional island the need to get away is hardly surprising. The only real cause for amazement is the number of people who seem quite content to live hugger-mugger with their neighbours and face the logjam of traffic every day.

Psychologists today define wanderlust as a kind of mental affliction. A dromomaniac is someone with "an abnormal, obsessive desire to roam." I prefer to call them people whose spirits perk up when they board the Heathrow express. The sister disorder, drapetomania, is even more challenging…"an uncontrollable urge to wander away from home."

These thoughts flashed through my mind as my companion described the doleful details of her broken romance. Looking back over a lifetime that had included several similar experiences I could only offer soothing words and trite remarks about more fish in the sea.

As carnival approached I began to stress out about my planned Cuban trip. In the travel agency I met a man from Corpus Christi, Texas who has been given the same run around by the charming Carl who liked to have his clients do all the work. I met the Texan later in the coffee shop-

"You take care y'all" were his parting words. I wondered how I would fare if I didn't take enough cash on the Cuban trip. I knew that Western credit cards could not be used on Fidel's island because of its pariah status and I was notoriously bad at arithmetic. I also fretted about leaving the country. Already, Mexico was beginning to feel like home.

The first night of the Carnival finally arrived and I stood for a punishing four hours watching the procession. It was good; not in the Notting Hill or Rio class but a charming small town version. I was chatted up relentlessly by a gigolo-type Mexican in excellent English.

'I love to meet women from the West; you are all so different and exciting. We Mayans are all the same!' Women nearby gave warning smiles and nods and the man eventually moved off when I proved unreceptive.

I could not boast of any romantic encounters on my trip. I don't think that Carl's invitation really qualified.

Isabella Bird, in her travels in the USA *(A Lady's Life in the Rocky Mountains)*, had her heart strings twanged by a dashing reprobate who declared his love for her. Strongly tempted to yield to his invitations she realised that he was not ideal marriage material and resumed her globe trotting.

I decided to miss the parade on the second day. In the local branch of Sanborn's I was intimidated into buying a paperback by Iain Banks at a very inflated price. The security guards did not allow browsing, but I was desperate for some reading matter. I finally managed to get some dollars and reported back to Carl at the agency. He told me that the British Ambassador was in town last night and he would have taken me along for a cocktail at the reception, but as he couldn't find me he had taken someone else.

I felt rather downcast at this news so he tried to cheer me up by suggesting that money could be made from buying old books in Cuba and selling them in the USA.

'I have a friend who is based in New Orleans who does very well at this. He travels the length and breadth of North America.' It didn't sound like a good career option for me so I headed back to the Trinidad where a group of German girls were complaining about mosquitoes. I had not been bitten so far, having relied on taking yeast tablets for two weeks before a trip - the mosquitoes hate the taste.

I discovered that I will have a four hour wait at the airport when I leave for Havana. I will have to leave the hotel early in order to get a taxi because the streets will be closed for the last carnival procession.

On departure day the taxi wended its way through crowds of revellers to reach the airport where I changed my remaining travellers' cheques at a bad rate. Time passed quickly because I chatted to the small, interesting group assembled for the flight. There were six of us in the deserted flight lounge, including a Leeds-born Canadian musician doing a wandering minstrel act around Latin America and a very nervous American lad hoping that Uncle Sam won't find out about his trip.

As we chatted, a small, red faced, unmistakeably English man in khaki shorts rushed into the lounge and begged us to take a parcel to Havana for him. He poured out a passionate story about his Cuban wife and child who were not allowed to join him in Merida. He shuttled back and forth whenever possible. Would we please take a parcel of necessities - ladies underwear and stuff for the child?

All this was uttered in broad Yorkshire tones while I looked on fascinated. The first rule of foreign travel is never accept parcels from strangers in airports but the man was so obvious in his manner that he could possibly be genuine.

In the end, the young American agreed to take the package while I gave him dire warnings about languishing in Cuban prisons for twenty years. The Yorkshireman disappeared and we were led away to our tiny, ancient plane which provoked much nervous laughter as it stood in solitary splendour on the runway. We barely had time to fasten our seatbelts before we were taking off. The cabin was un-pressurised and we suffered accordingly. Two Canadians swore softly as their ears popped.

The handsome steward and stewardess were friendly and apologetic, handing out sweets, Cuban beer and stale sandwiches- a taste of things to come, no doubt.

18
Cuba - "This isn't a Tale of Derring Do"
The Motorcycle Diaries

When the plane finally touched down at Jose Marti airport it was ten p.m. The place was swarming with officials but we were the only passengers. After being processed I walked out of the airport buildings into total darkness. The black, tropical night swallowed me instantly, as if I had leapt into a vat of warm Guinness. There was no sign of any taxis, although we had been told that some were available.

As I stood, irresolute, clutching my bag, a young lad of about fourteen appeared out of the night and pointed to a dilapidated saloon just visible in the gloom. I was invited to travel into Havana in this vehicle - his seventeen year old brother would drive.

'Only fifteen dollars, much cheaper than official taxi,' the boy said, seizing my bag. I threw caution to the winds and followed him. As the car drove onto the highway the youths asked me politely if I would mind lying down in the back and covering myself with a blanket in case any policeman were watching. They apologised profusely for this indignity saying there were 'Muchas problemas en Cuba.' I discovered later that unofficial taxis were banned but anyone with a car tried to earn money this way. The Cuban currency was worthless and the beleaguered Habañeros were desperate to earn dollars.

We trundled over roads with gaping potholes and stopped eventually near the Hotel Deauville on the Malécon, the broad boulevard overlooking the harbour. I passed fifteen dollars to the boys who bowed elegantly and carried my bag to the steps of the hotel.

My experience of the curiously empty plane trip from Merida was not dissimilar to Margaret Fountaine's experience when she returned to Cuba on a half empty ship. It was just after the Wall Street crash of 1932 and the hotels of Havana were free of tourists. She *"spent most of the winter inexpensively in Guantanamo"* - not something she would wish to do these days.

The resolute and infinitely susceptible Miss Fountaine could cope with anything except storms at sea. She saw off drunken miners who barged into her tent or cabin and remained stoic during a Cuban earthquake.

One evening...I could not help noticing the strange behaviour of the dog Jock. He seemed worried about something and was never still a moment. That night I could not sleep; I felt the strangest foreboding, and I was still wide awake when soon after midnight the whole building shook as with an earthquake. The hotel was largely composed of wood, and I felt little or no fear, not even when the lights went out. But it was over and I was soon so sound asleep that another, though not quite as severe shock at about 5a.m. failed to wake me. The earthquake had wrecked Santiago. Everyone now seemed at high tension, always in anticipation of another shock, but Jock and I knew the worst was over.

It is strange how animals always seem to know when an earthquake is coming. I afterwards heard that the horses in the corral had also been greatly disturbed that evening, and when the shock actually came they all went down on their knees until it was over.

The horses did the sensible thing. When I was caught in the shower during one of San Francisco's famous strong tremors many years ago I remained upright, naked, with water gushing over me as the cubicle tilted sharply. Paralysed with fear, I remember thinking that this was such an undignified way to die.

Once inside the Deauville I found it was a huge,

Communist-style building swarming with tourists and a large number of exceptionally surly staff. Vouchers had to be obtained before one could eat breakfast and artificial orange juice was served. Real oranges were exported; one of the few items that Cuba could sell, along with cigars.

My room was fine, up on the sixteenth floor with a good view of the city, but I knew I could not afford to stay long. I needed to find somewhere cheaper and I wanted to find a way to reach the famed colonial city of Trinidad on the other side of the island.

My first stop next day was the Cubanatour office, which proved to be a dispiriting experience. I temporarily abandoned trying to get to Trinidad and settled for a tourist bus trip to a place called Sancti Spiritus. The Cubanatour official, who must have been trained by the KGB, took my thirteen dollars for the trip while explaining that no hotel reservations could be made for Trinidad because the computer couldn't cope - a strange excuse, I thought, even with my limited knowledge of IT. I asked about a simple telephone call but she became hard of hearing.

Her colleague told me that it was not "advisable" for tourists to travel alone on buses and trains. I knew that bus travel was difficult because of the lack of fuel but I wondered what that endlessly elastic word advisable meant in this context. Public transport was paid for in local currency and tourists were only allowed to spend dollars...as in "strongly advised."

It was all too reminiscent of Communist Eastern Europe where officials were always telling you that anything you wanted to do was forbidden. No explanations were ever forthcoming. I sat on a hot, hairy sofa idly glancing at the leaflet describing the tour. It promised wonderful scenery along with the inevitable visit to a cigar factory. Nearby another middle-aged, middle-class, English sex tourist was complaining loudly about lost cash and his inability to find a chica for the night. I slunk quietly out into the midday sun as my fellow-countryman demanded that the guide find him a 'Hot, coloured number.' He wasn't referring to a Hawaiian T-shirt.

He would probably be luckier than I was in my attempts to travel or find the ice cream I craved. Seconds later the official appeared at the door and called after me not to be late for the bus tomorrow. I wished I could think of something cutting in Spanish but I could only conjure up an all-purpose Italian obscenity

I trudged up the hill towards the former Hilton hotel, now renamed the Havana Libre, dodging the street people who can recognise a tourist at several hundred paces. The amount of hassle on the streets of Havana was phenomenal. If you walked anywhere or sat in a park they appeared out of the woodwork. My small, dark, middle-aged woman-fits-in-everywhere persona was no use here.

'Would you like some cigars, special price...a taxi, unofficial, very cheap, can I show you a good time, buy your T shirt, sell you my sister?'

I know they are desperate people but there is none of the dignity that the equally poor and exploited Mexican Indians have as they appear at your side mutely offering something hand crafted and beautiful. A refusal is usually met with a bow and a polite goodbye. A refusal here is received with mixed incredulity and hostility. Cuba is into the hard sell and the currency is mainly bodies and, of course, dollars.

In a park near the hotel I rested my feet while keeping watch on a nearby kiosk. It advertised ice cream and it appeared to be open, but the absence of queues was a bad sign. I had not eaten fruit since I arrived in Havana and as I scuffed my sandals in the dust I wondered how long it took to develop the symptoms of scurvy.

Earlier I had attempted to find the market that I knew existed in the city but whenever I asked a local for directions they would look vague and say that it was faraway, "Muy lejos," as they waved a hand in the general direction of Miami. Perhaps it was **in** Miami. Once I had seen a man selling gnarled and ancient grapefruits on a street corner, but otherwise, nothing.

Eventually, curiosity overcame me and I went over to the kiosk that was staffed by two bored-looking girls. They explained that ice cream was rationed which I already knew and, alas, it was not their day for a delivery.

'Come back on Thursday, early,' they advised. 'Get here before the queues begin. Tourists don't need ration books.' They waved as I walked away. I wondered why they had bothered to come to work if they had nothing to sell; Castro probably insisted. My mother would have loved this place - backs to the wall, ration books, and queues for everything - just like World War Two.

After a couple of days in the hotel it was essential that I found somewhere cheaper to stay. As I wandered around the streets I noticed another palabar, one of the private homes where the ground floor front room had been turned into a restaurant. Castro now turns a blind eye to these endeavours as the economy continues to sink.

I stopped at one window and started talking to Rosario, a tall, distinguished older woman with waist length dreadlocks. She told me that she had taught English at the university until they stopped paying the salaries. Now she cooked for a living. Enticing smells crept from the back kitchen into the living area which was the restaurant.

Rosario's children and grandchildren milled around and a group of neighbours played cards at a corner table. An arthritic fan circled slowly overhead barely stirring the lace curtains dividing the rooms. I was reminded of my grandmother's post-war house, cosy and welcoming despite the lack of mod cons. Even the lace curtain was the same. I asked Rosario if she knew of a cheap place to stay and she told me that she had a friend nearby who rented a room. She would speak to her and I should come back tomorrow.

I continued my wandering around the streets, absorbing the feel of Havana and worrying about fruit. In the Museum of the Revolution the dusty remnants of Cuba's moments of glory were on display, a tattered Stars and Stripes, an American plane shot down during the Bay of Pigs episode. I remembered that time when the world held its breath while the USA and Soviet Russia faced each other across a nuclear abyss.

Pictures of Che Guevara were everywhere, the wild, handsome face that had adorned my student bedroom and thousands of others, the perfect revolutionary. 'Hasta La Victoria Siempre'…Forever, until Victory, shouted the slogans on the walls.

An even bigger memorial to Che dominated the Plaza de la Revolucion overshadowing the man who was Cuba's hero in pre-Castro/Guevara days. The poet Jose Marti, who gave his name to Havana's airport, was the original father of Cuban Independence in the late 19th century and, like Che Guevara, he died young in the early stages of the struggle against Spain. Copies of his poetry were prominent on the second hand book stalls.

As I walked down a street near the museum I spotted a sign indicating an Arab cultural centre linked to one of the few countries maintaining relations with Cuba in the face of Uncle Sam's disapproval. Fortunately, the EC is strong enough to be defiant. Many EC countries, especially Spain, fund projects on the island, particularly in the tourism sector.

As long as the American embargo continues tourism will be the only thing keeping Cuba's economy afloat. New hotels were springing up from Varadero right along the coast as more and more Europeans and Canadians poured in. The experience of being on a Caribbean island devoid of US citizens was one to be savoured. The few who defied the ban were usually worth meeting.

At that very moment I rounded a corner and saw the young American from the plane walking with a tall, thin, sharply dressed Cuban whose pin-striped suit and fedora made him seem the epitome of a 1950s gangster. The American had lost his nervousness and introduced me to Jose who was showing him around and taking him to all the 'cool' places for a mere ten dollars a day. This sum together with commissions from cigar selling and the sex industry probably meant that Jose was a local millionaire.

After another uncomfortable and expensive night at the Deauville I reported back to Rosario's place and ate one of her fried fish meals with black beans and rice. There is no gourmet cooking in Cuba. The same men played cards and the small brown children scampered under the tables.

Afterwards we walked to Rosario's friend's place in a street with the usual gaping potholes and absence of street lighting. We entered a small apartment house and found Catalina on the third floor with her husband and fourteen-year old son. They slept downstairs in a friend's home so that their bedroom could be rented to tourists. Catalina handed me her card that boasted "hot water always" which would prove to be pure fiction, but at fifteen dollars a night it seemed like a bargain compared with the hotel.

The room was clean and the bed comfortable enough. There was no glass in the windows but this was a useful cooling device in a building without air-conditioning. The noise from the street was tremendous but I was usually too tired to care. It was agreed that I would move in on the following day.

'When the Austrian leaves' said Catalina. Beds in Cuba never get cold.

During the time I stayed at the apartment I developed a strange, fraught relationship with my hostess. She often went out with me in the evening to act as my guide. We would drink negritos and mojitos in open air bars free of tourists. She told me about her mother who had been a political prisoner for several years before fleeing to the US. Catalina hated Castro with a passion. During my time in Havana I never heard anyone praise him. Most people said they were waiting for him to die, something he showed no sign of doing.

Ordinary Cubans wanted to be led into bondage in Coca-Cola land, willingly sacrificing their principles for the coveted US standard of living or a fraction of it. They would lose as much, if not more than they gained, but when you lack even the basic amenities principles don't stand a chance. Cuba wanted to be a kept woman, snatching a slice of the good life before it was too late. Few of its citizens were old enough to remember what Cuba was like before Castro when Havana was a city-size brothel for North America. The enormous gains made in education and health were ranged against the reality of the blockade.

'Cubans are f..........!' remarked Catalina's husband cheerfully. 'We can do only what the Americans allow. If you can't beat them..........'

Catalina took me to the huge Spanish cemetery on the way to the residential district of Vedado where the politicians and diplomats live. She pointed out the tombs of voodoo priestesses, saying that she herself was catholic but that santeria was influential on the island. As we walked around she launched into a tirade against the sex tourists, many of whom are paedophiles, alleging, 'I would shoot them all!'

In my head I called Catalina and her husband the two Billies. Physically, my hostess reminded me of pictures I had seen of the American singer Billie Holliday, and her husband looked very much like the actor Bill Cosby. In general, Cubans are an extraordinarily handsome people, a fortuitous blending of African, Spanish and several other strains.

As we drove past the beautiful seaside villas where

American movie stars used to spend the winter I thought of the Hemingway era. Marooned in no-man's-land these exquisite homes and estates that would be worth millions by Caribbean standards are almost worthless.

Catalina wanted her son to study English and computer technology so that he could conquer the world. When I offered to send some text-books from England her manner changed subtly. Often she veered from friendliness to anger, but offers of help seemed to make her resentful

'I suppose you enjoy helping poor black Habañeros?' she would sneer. I said nothing but I left most of my medical kit behind as a peace offering. Medicines are now in as short supply as everything else on the island.

I offered to forward letters to her mother in San Francisco but Catalina just changed the subject. It seemed that only my American dollars could be accepted unconditionally. I began to wonder how much of her story was true and how much was invented for my benefit. The Byzantine complexities of life under a Communist régime are unimaginable to most Westerners.

On the day Catalina told me that she was expecting a second child I accompanied the whole family into the centre to visit friends. We travelled in a neighbour's beat-up jalopy that functioned as an unofficial taxi. We had barely reached the Hotel Inglaterra where I was to be dropped off when the car was stopped by police officers who were having a random crack down on unlicensed vehicles.

As a tourist I was carefully ignored, but everyone else had to report to the police station. Later, Catalina told me that the driver and her husband, Marti, were kept in the cells for two days. She and her son were questioned for several hours and they were only allowed to leave when she told them she was pregnant.

The following day was my scheduled trip to Sancti Spiritus and I obediently scurried along the Malécon at eight am in the early morning with hazy sunshine lazily overseeing the blue green sea and small boys diving off the rocks. I was greeted cheerily by a few fishermen and returning revellers. I arrived panting at the entrance to one of Havana's most expensive hotels where the minibus was waiting.

My companions consisted of assorted, gilded Eurotrash - several cheerful, perfumed Spanish women from Valencia, two gay Italians wearing a great deal of gold and Versace, a morose Frenchman, a pleasant Greek couple and moi - the only Brit and the only unaccompanied female.

Our guide was a beautiful young woman with full KGB mannerisms who announced that she didn't speak English. Everyone looked at me and I immediately plunged into a conversation with the Spanish ladies to show that I was not a monoglot English barbarian. We sped out of the city while the Valencian ladies and I agreed that the Cuban Spanish accent was difficult to understand.

Apart from the forced visit to another cigar factory the trip was enjoyable, giving a glimpse of the tobacco growing interior of the island and the curious rock formations similar to those in Guangxi, China.

Back in Havana I retreated once again to the Hotel Inglaterra where, joy of joys, strawberry icecream was available and the pianist tinkled Chopin under the palms.

I finally accepted that I would not get to the town of Trinidad by public transport and made arrangements to visit Ernest Hemingway's house instead. This involved lengthy discussions with my hosts who sent their young son to the house of a neighbour called Rolando who had a "reliable" vehicle that would take me to the place in comfort for only fifteen dollars.

I knew what a reliable car meant in this part of the world; probably the back end of a 1956 Chevy welded to the front end of a 1970s Lada. This was unimportant compared with the difficulty of avoiding the police who were constantly on the lookout for unauthorised taxis driven by would-be capitalists who were undermining the pure Communist ethos of Fidel's island.

My hostess assured me that Rolando had sufficient charm and low cunning to be a match for the police. He had once been an important official in the régime and knew Fidel well, until he had become disillusioned. Catalina told me this as we ate the usual rice and beans with a little chopped egg early one evening before the power cuts started. I decided that he had probably been Fidel's chauffeur at some time.

Young Jose came back saying that everything had been arranged for tomorrow. Rolando's apartment was just around the corner and he would wait for me. Jose then gave a huge grin and brought in the bucket of warm water he had carried back for me.

I almost cried with gratitude; after a few days on this island in the dust and humidity of the city, a bucket of warm water represented the height of civilisation. As I rushed into the bathroom Catalina called out that Rolando would treat me like a queen. Of course he would, I reminded myself; fifteen dollars was almost the equivalent of a month's wages in these parts.

When I met the man I was ashamed of my cynicism. He was as handsome and charming as Catalina had promised and he handed me into his worn but still well preserved saloon with its gleaming tail fins as if I was a movie star. We agreed that I would pretend to be his wife if we were stopped by the police, but we drove to San Francisco de Paula, about two and a half kilometres from central Havana, without any problems. Rolando told me stories of his days on Fidel's payroll and then shrugged his shoulders.

'Nothing will change while the old man lives - and he's immortal!'

Hemingway's house was a large villa or finca gleaming white in the sun. In the carefully tended garden his boat was on display, its woodwork and brass work polished to a golden shimmer. The graves of his pet dogs were near the empty swimming pool.

One of Havana's well-informed guides showed me around the house, another girl beautiful enough to star in Hollywood. The old MCP's study was just as he left it with his hunting trophies on display on the bookshelves. Even the cat was a direct descendant of the one Hemingway had kept.

Later, Rolando drove me back, kissed my hand and promised to drive me to the airport when I left, 'For only sixteen dollars.' He said we would have to pretend to be related in case the police were watching. He would give me a passionate embrace just to be on the safe side. It seemed an unlikely scenario to me. Everyone knew that Cubans couldn't fly anywhere.

'You are my cousin living in London,' he said firmly, and I wasn't going to disagree. This man was easily the most attractive man I had met on my travels, except for Carl, the perfidious French-Canadian travel agent.

One day I took the ferry ride across the bay from La Fuerza castle to Casablanca and La Regla, two villages that offer a little respite from the crowds and dusty streets of Havana. The fare was fifty centavos, probably the only bargain to be had in the city - if you are a tourist.

I sat in a small, grassy playground where a solitary child played with a small dog. Shaded by palm trees I wrote notes and savoured the peace. A wander around the little town revealed a beautiful church that the locals were restoring. The churches were often well preserved but I had never seen a priest or a service going on. The façade of one Spanish colonial church in the capital resembled a castellated, snow-white wedding cake. An armed man stood guard outside and waved me in with his rifle.

When I left the church to look for a cold drink I was followed by a small boy about eight years old who offered to be my guide. He took me to a bar near the station where I bought two cokes for us, the real Coca-Cola, not the Cuban imitation.

We were soon surrounded by his friends, three ragged urchins who stared in disbelief and longing as my guide clutched his red and silver can. I wondered if he would ever drink it or whether he would keep it as a souvenir, a symbol of all that was unattainable for most people in this country.

Later I travelled back to the city on the ferry where returning workers flirted with me while others snogged each other passionately on the benches. Sex is the only free, available activity for Cuba's poor, although Rosario had told me that couples often rented motel rooms by the hour to gain some privacy in this overcrowded city. She smiled and shrugged saying,

'Cubans are, how do you say in English... as randy as rabbits!'

On my wanderings around the city my favourite spot in the old town was the Plaza de Armas with the beautiful Palace of the Captains General, now the city museum, and the nearby Museum of Colonial Art. Formerly the palace of a Spanish grandee, the latter was a gem, full of graceful, colonial furniture painted deep blue and white, with lace curtains billowing at the windows in the tropical breeze. The room sets were beautifully arranged and I expected the family to enter at any moment. I had the place to myself, watched by the usual bored, benign female attendants.

In the cathedral, popularly known as the Columbus, Christopher's bones have been removed. After Cuban Independence they were taken to Seville, although Santo Domingo in the Dominican Republic also claims to have them. No-one seems to know whether the bones are Christopher's or those of one of his relatives.

I wandered back to say goodbye to my hosts before heading to the airport with Rolando, but not before doing the full tourist Monty by having a Mojito at Hemingway's bar, forcing my way through the tourist throng.

At the airport I bade an affectionate farewell to Rolando who had somehow become my best friend, if not my boyfriend, in a short space of time. The officials standing around the terminal looked unusually tense but I thought nothing of it; I was looking forward to getting back 'home' to Merida. Little did I realise that Uncle Sam had some ideas about that.

19
Izamal-Tulum- Gods and Devils

The Americans had chosen that day to for some anti-Castro action. One of their planes was menacing a Cuban airforce plane over the narrow stretch of water between Havana and the Yucatan. Fortunately, they did not bother with our small aircraft and we landed unaware of what might have happened to us

Soon after my return to Merida I visited the nearby town of Izamal because I had been told that it was more authentically Mayan, and less tourist-ridden than the state capital.

I found myself inside a life-size gingerbread town - small, Colonial houses painted yellow and adorned with what looked like marzipan gilding. The town was dominated by the largest Franciscan convent in the world (reputedly), which houses the shrine of Our Lady of Izamal, Patron of the Yucatan. The statue of the Virgin had beautiful but distinctly European features. The nuns were long gone; religious orders were suppressed after one of Mexico's many revolutions, but the Pope had visited the shrine in 1993 and the town has not yet recovered. There were photographs of John Paul 11 everywhere and the buildings received another coat of yellow paint.

The convent had been built on the site of some Mayan ruins and to the left of the convent lay the pyramid called Kinich-Kakmo, the fifth highest in the country. When I tried to climb it I was told that the entrance was through an adjoining tortilla factory and the premises were firmly closed. It was siesta time.

Izamal was an important Mayan centre until the Spanish arrived. A memorial in the town spells out the ambiguous feelings of the Mayan people and their misgivings about the Columbus celebrations. The statue was of Fray Diego de Landa, a Franciscan missionary who built the convent and destroyed the Mayan religion in the process. The inscription described him as – "Light and dark, destroyer and builder, historian and law-giver, persecutor of the Indians." The statue dated from 1971.

In the empty white square in front of the convent pretty horse drawn carriages were lined up waiting for the tourists who were seldom around at this time of year. I hired one and we clip-clopped slowly around sleepy streets almost buried in tropical vegetation. At one point the horse stopped and appeared to fall asleep for a few moments while his driver nodded off in sympathy.

In the market most of the older women did not speak Spanish and giggled helplessly when I tried to communicate to them. The Mayan language appeared on street names and public signs. I ate lunch in a hidden courtyard restaurant with a Canadian couple, obsessive explorers of Mayan ruins, who came to the Yucatan every winter. We ate my favourite fish dish, red snapper in a spicy tomato sauce – huachinango.

Frances Calderon de la Barca called this style of cooking "Spanish Vera-Crucified" and thought it very unpalatable....*garlic and oil enveloping meat, fish and fowl, with pimentos and plantains and all kinds of curious fruit that I cannot yet endure.*

In the 1930s the globe trotting journalist, Rosita Forbes, finally left aside her passion for the Middle East and travelled to South and Central America with her husband. Her reactions to the Yucatan were similar to my own.

It was oven hot when we landed at Merida. The ground seemed to take deliberate pleasure in discomfiting me. It retreated and advanced in burning waves. The sand was so hot that it stabbed through my thin soles...-a strange reaction from someone who had survived the dreadful crossing of the Sahara to the Kufra oasis.

Later I fell in love with Mexico because of its indomitable character and the way it takes its beauties for granted, as well as for the simplicity of the half-Indian peoples, the courage of its obstinate and always- being- murdered patriots and the gorgeous over decoration of its churches and landscapes.

It is incomparable in its contrasts-dark pine forests and tawny, leonine deserts, Mayan temples, prodigious as the ideas of midnight, and the plains of Puebla breaking into highly coloured domes like soap bubbles.

I took the rattle-trap bus back to Merida, a journey of one and a half hours through beautiful citrus plantations, before collapsing gratefully in the cool, palm-shrouded Hotel Trinidad. I pondered whether I had enough energy to go around the corner to the sister hotel for a swim in the pool, but at that point I fell asleep.

The Trinidad stays in my mind as the perfect resting place for the oddball, budget traveller. My room was the most attractive of any I stayed in at any price level. One wall had a large reproduction of a Manet Impressionist garden and the adjoining shower room was always pristine. The room's window overlooked the courtyard which was tree-shrouded and full of potted plants and old-fashioned rattan furniture from the 1930s.

There were few guests at that time of year despite the crowds in the town centre and the whole place had that air of indefinable melancholy that slightly seedy hotels out of season often have. The senora was always on duty, impassive yet benevolent. Various friends and relatives visited her and her small dog lay across the desk, opening one eye when guests arrived. Staff seldom appeared, but the room was always clean and fresh towels were supplied daily. There were no other services but budget travellers cater for themselves.

I could have lived there quite happily for a few months. There was a place to write on the veranda and I was disturbed only occasionally by German backpackers who are plentiful at any time of year. The faint sounds of the town drifted over the treetops, a police siren or the screams of fighting cats, but generally the silence was unbroken despite the proximity to the town centre. I think it was the combination of tropical inertia and companionable regret that really appealed to me.

My time in the Yucatan was coming to an end and I was determined to make an expedition to some Mayan ruins that were not tourist infested. I met an Englishwoman in town who agreed to go with me to the ruins of Tulum, about 131 kilometres south of Cancun. Although less popular than Chichen-Itza, even this sight is now very much visited. Eventually, we found a way to have the place to ourselves.

Helen, my companion for this trip, was another civil servant like the one I had met in Oaxaca, who was taking time off from her career- 'Some me time,' as she put it. There must be something about the dessicated air of those corridors of power that cause its employees to burn out at some stage

Her pale blonde bob was lightly streaked with grey, the only indication of her forty plus years. She had bright blue eyes and a fearless gaze honed from dealing with politicians of all shades. After travelling in Costa Rica and Mexico she planned to whale watch in Baja California.

Helen's practical, can do air convinced this reluctant swimmer and night time hater that we could tackle a nocturnal expedition successfully, with some help from resident North Americans and local Mayans. I invoked the spirit of Mary Kingsley as we left.

It was approaching midnight when we set out across the beach heading for the grey-black ruins of Mexico's past;

Tulum was bathed in shimmering moonlight almost as bright as the tropical sun.

We had spent the latter part of the afternoon familiarising ourselves with the layout of the city in the forest that had once guarded this part of the Yucatan peninsula against invasion from the sea. Now we were eager to see the ruins free from the day time hordes of fluorescent -clad tourists from Cancun, further up the coast where the Caribbean merges into the Gulf of Mexico.

We were fully aware of the dubious nature of our expedition. The ruins are off-limits at night and well guarded. Whilst Mexican laws are enforced only when the breaking of them is construed as a threat, it is not the gringo's place to exploit the turn-a blind-eye syndrome unnecessarily. For this reason we decided to enter the site from the shoreline rather than risk an encounter with the authorities who could be safely bribed with tequila if one was a local, but who demanded hard currency and plausible excuses from foreigners.

The tide was already quite high as we set out across the base of the cliff face and the seasonal winds tested our concentration and agility at every step. I was uncomfortably aware of the seven varieties of scorpions, a multitude of tarantulas, enormous iguanas, the odd jaguar and deadly coral snakes underfoot. Luckily the high winds tended to drive the assorted beasties further inland. At least I had not had time to reflect on whether I was getting too old for this sort of thing.

Eventually, we climbed up to the edge of the jungle and reached the ruins. Helen had become more determined as we struggled along whereas I, typically, had started out full of false bravado and had become progressively more terrified.

The ruins of Tulum have a magical setting on the edge of the jungle bounded by the white sand beach and the turquoise Caribbean. Now the towers stood out black in the bright moonlight and the star-filled sky was a deep mauve as we climbed the pyramid-like staircase to the summit of the tallest building. Below us the luminous sea stretched into the night.

El Castillo, named by the conquistadors who reached Tulum three quarters of a century before it was abandoned, was a temple dedicated to the god of the full moon, Noh Ehk. As I sat beneath a stone carving of the god the ancient stones stood defined against the dusty earth casting strange shadows across the enclosure. Beyond the walls, seven metres thick and as intact as the day they were built stretched the green, pulsing, omnivorous jungle extending as far as the eye could see and farther than the mind can imagine. Pinpoints of light from the surrounding naval bases broke the blanket of vegetation at intervals and scarcely disturbed the sense of timelessness.

I tried to imagine the fear and wonder of the inhabitants as they sighted the sails of the first Spanish ships on the horizon. It felt as if the city had been deserted only hours before and we were the last people to leave this outpost of civilisation.

In Mayan legend, Tulum, at that time known as Zama was visited by two philosopher pilgrims, Keh and Antzab. They brought sacrificial offerings of jade and pom, a type of incense made from aromatic resin. They arrived on the day following the full moon and in self-sacrifice pierced their ears and tongue.

As the blood flowed, the goddess of the new moon, Ixchel, sent down her blessing. The description given of Tulum was comprehensive; it was completed in 433AD. At that time there were fifty buildings standing but the city's population was minimal, consisting only of important male officials who made political and religious decisions concerning the outlying settlements.

At the time of the chroniclers' arrival a festival dedicated to the war god, Pacum Chac, was taking place. They witnessed the sacrificial offering of the hearts of virgins to Cit Chac Coh; the dismembering took place on the upper platform of El Castillo.

As I thought about the history of the stones around me the eeriness of the place was increased by the weird sounds of a drunken Mayan singing to the full moon from deep inside the temple. The wailing cries disturbed the guard dogs and brought the terrified guard himself, a stick in one hand and a gun in the other. He was obviously relieved to see gringos and locals and not the unhappy spirits of past victims.

He relaxed somewhat and politely ordered us down, his authoritative 'Bajense' lost in the now howling wind.

We beat a hasty retreat back through the jungle only to find that the tide was high when we reached the cliff. The moon had clouded over and the return trip became dark, wet and dangerous. I am just an ageing romantic and a scribbler, not a wild adventurer I reminded myself as I wept with fright in the unmerciful darkness.

We arrived, sodden, bruised and exhausted back at the beach camp. I felt humbled when I looked at my sorry state and remembered travellers like Ella Christie pushing through inhospitable territory with only her Indian sandals, dark glasses and cherry brandy to keep her warm. I could not lay my hands on anything but some warm coca cola.

After a soothing night in a hammock – the perfect way to sleep, I recovered my spirits and decided that the Yucatan fascinated me more than any other part of Mexico. Perhaps I had been nipped by a Chacmool* in a previous life.

The local population at Tulum was small and outnumbered by a flourishing hippy community, mainly Americans and Canadians. They were happy to act as guides if you wanted to see the cenotes, the deep fresh-water pits like lakes in the jungle. The local Mayans offered us the illegal black coral jewellery and langosta (crayfish), also illegal because it was out of season.

After the obligatory tours of other greater and lesser ruins, Teotihuacan, Palenque, Chichen Itza etc, Tulum was a delight. Its remote position almost on the border with Belize and twenty-five hours by road from Mexico City has saved it from over-exploitation.

This was the land of the descending god; his image was carved in stone at Tulum - a country still touched by gods and devils, full of delight and horror, beauty and pollution, in the past as in the present. Cortes was wrong, New Spain it is not.

* Chacmool - a reclining statue of a Mayan deity awaiting offerings.

20
Merida-Taxco – The Honorary Consul

My next adventure or rather, mishap, back in Merida was due entirely to my own carelessness. Later, I consoled myself with the knowledge that even the most intrepid lady traveller occasionally found herself in a tight spot.

After returning from Tulum I bought a ticket for my onward journey at Merida's small bus station and then wandered back into the centre of town leaving my shoulder bag unzipped. The only time I let my guard slip. A trio of fierce-looking Indian men passed by brushing close to me and when I arrived back in town and tried to buy a cold drink I discovered that my wallet was gone and with it all my cash, my credit card and ticket.

Panic swept over me as I realised that I was far from the Embassy and friends in Mexico City with no access to money at all and no shelter for the night. I sat on a low wall by the cathedral and gave way to despair for a few moments. Of course, I was not thinking straight. I could have asked the people at the Hotel Trinidad to make a call for me. They would probably even have given me a room.

A woman stopped and asked if she could help me. Compassionate strangers exist in the most unlikely places. She was a small, slight Afro-American; fluent in Spanish and able to sooth my rising hysteria. Together we retraced my steps and she persuaded the bus officials to re-issue my ticket. Sanity clicked in at that point and I remembered that there was an honorary British consul in Merida. My compassionate stranger gave me the coins to make a call and paid for a taxi to the consul's house, waving away my voluble thanks with a smile. We had not exchanged names or addresses, it was a very brief encounter, but I hoped that she would visit England one day and that we would meet again and I could repay the kindness.

The honorary consul sounded elderly and somewhat peeved when he answered the phone. It was Sunday evening and he obviously resented being disturbed by travellers who were careless enough to get themselves robbed.

As I stood on his doorstep, distraught and sweating, the heavy oak doors swung open to reveal a man who looked about one hundred years old with a white beard that reached almost to his knees. Apart from telling me to call him major he said nothing but beckoned me to follow him. As I struggled with my bags I wondered which war he had fought in - the Boer War probably. What did I expect? I wasn't even a tax payer

Moments later I was in a cool, tiled room drinking a long, cold drink while the consul's wife fussed over me. She seemed considerably younger than her husband who re-appeared with a slightly younger version of himself, with a slightly shorter beard - his brother.

The trio listened politely while I told my tale of woe. The consul/major remarked that people should never travel alone and that travellers were constantly disappearing without trace in Mexico. Thus reassured I was led into the high tech office which contrasted strongly with the general 1950s air of the house.

A fax machine spewed out tales of disaster direct from the Embassy in the capital. I was allowed to call my daughter in Scotland to arrange for a transfer of funds. The major kept tut-tutting about 'the cost of all this.' I couldn't believe that his expenses were not covered; perhaps I should make a donation to that worthy charity the British Exchequer when I returned home.

The four of us ate a meal while I tried to keep awake and nod politely as the major's tales of travellers' mishaps grew ever more lurid. Eventually, his wife told him to play the piano to shut him up. She started to tell me the family history while the major played the hits of the 1940s on an elderly instrument suffering from tropical lassitude.

Mrs Major obviously relished having another woman around. The brother uttered not a word and the major played on until he fell asleep across the piano. Nobody moved.

The major had been born in the Yucatan to Anglo-Spanish parents. Educated in England where he trained as an engineer, he returned to England to fight in the War. In 1946 he brought his new wife back to Merida. She was from the Home Counties and spoke no Spanish. The town at that time was just a small Indian settlement where all food had to be bought in the local market. The heat was crushing.

'You just have to take an aspirin and lie down, my dear.'

They had watched the town grow and modernise with some distaste, but for both of them time had stopped in the 1950s. They had not been back to Britain for decades and had no idea about the realities of life in the present day UK. The major had been the consul since the 1940s and his father before him.

Mrs Major was kindness personified and I sank gratefully into bed in their guest room between lavender-scented sheets.

When I surfaced the next morning I found the consul shaving himself on the balcony and his wife waving to me from the garden in her very Home Counties floral dress. After breakfast I discovered that she had removed my clothes from my room and had them washed and ironed.

I felt embarrassed by my meagre wardrobe, now fairly threadbare at this stage of the journey. Those Victorian women would have felt that I was letting the side down.

Mrs Alec Tweedie, author of the triumphantly titled *Tight Corners of my Adventurous Life,* was a handsome woman who liked to be photographed at home in ribbons and lace, but when in a tight corner somewhere her divided skirts retained their knife-edged crease. In marked contrast to my own appearance in Mexico she wore a black riding habit, white ruffled shirts and a sombrero. This outfit, in which she rode, hunted and shot with aplomb caused consternation among Mexican gentlemen who had never seen such a sight.

In general, Victorian women travellers, even if not as sartorially splendid as Mrs Tweedie, knew the importance of keeping up appearances. Corsets had to be worn, even in darkest Africa, *"because there is something about their absence almost as demoralising as hair in curling pins."*(Mary Kingsley). What would she have thought of overweight American women shopping in hair rollers and Bermuda shorts?

I set off to retrieve money from Thomas Cook, returning to collect my luggage and to thank my hosts for their hospitality. Mrs Major bade me a warm farewell while the consul wondered aloud whether I had 'learned my lesson.' I decided this was not the moment to mention Mary Kingsley crossing Africa alone, resolute in her corset.

I set off for the bus station once more, suitably chastened and without a credit card for the rest of the trip.

The bus journey to Taxco meandered through spectacular scenery, snow-capped mountains, hairpin bends, green fields and flower-filled villages with the locals in their Sunday best thronging the streets. The bus was half empty and I chatted in Spanglish to a woman who was on her way back to Acapulco.

The silver city must be the prettiest in Mexico. From the church of Santa Prisca with its ornate, pale rose coloured façade and tiled dome to the candy coloured houses perched on the hills and the riotous colours of the local market, the whole place is a feast for the eyes. Unfortunately, the same could not be said for the hotel where I decided to perch for a day or two. Misnamed the Grande its advantage was that it was close to the centre, the disadvantages were - everything else. Situated in a colonial building that crumbled as you watched, there was a huge central courtyard with galleries above where the cell-like rooms were situated. The drains smelled horrible, the bathroom was dirty and the nightclub situated at ground level usually made sleep impossible.

The zocolo was alive with balloon sellers and vendors of straw hats, tourists, expats and silver buyers from everywhere. The silver mines here provided a river of wealth for the Spanish and the town is famous for its silver work today. I wandered through dozens of shops, eventually treating myself to a bangle.

The handiwork on display in the market was astounding; textiles, ceramics and artwork, all intensely covetable. I had to break off my explorations for the usual chores - finding a laundry and a cheap place to eat. I took a collective taxi known as a combi up the vertical street called Panoramica to get a view of the volcanoes but they were hidden by smog or mist. My fellow passengers were jolly Mexican housewives laden with shopping bags. Why was I the only gringa ever seen in a collective taxi?

I planned to visit the waterfalls of Acuitlapan which were about twenty one kilometres from the town. I had read that donkeys were available to take you down to the falls from the village. I was suffering from a slight attack of the Turista that I attributed to the unsanitary conditions at the hotel and I was not at my best when I got off the bus at the village which seemed to consist of one run-down cantina where two women were serving alcohol to a few burly peasants. I enquired about hiring burros and said I wanted to visit the falls. I had not seen any donkeys in the adjoining fields but they could not be far away, I reasoned.

My request as greeted with consternation by the locals. It was definitely NOT safe for a lone senora, I was assured. I asked about a guide but they shook their heads. There were no donkeys available and the path was unsafe.

"Why?" I asked. The men muttered and looked shifty. Finally one said emphatically that there were snakes and it was definitely unsafe, 'For the senora.'

I never discovered whether it was my deathly pallor or some other reason that prompted them to get rid of me as soon as possible. A free can of coke was pressed into my hand while another man flagged down a combi that materialised unexpectedly on the deserted road. I was grabbed and lifted into it by the two men who commanded the driver to 'Take the senora straight back to Taxco.'

My imagination went into overdrive as we bowled along. Were the men operating some kind of illicit racket down at the falls? The story about the snakes was possibly true but the place was written up in the tourist guides after all. I decided that they were prompted by compassion for my sickly appearance, or a possible shortage of donkeys. It was just as well; I was really feeling under the weather. I returned to the unhealthy hotel, dosed myself and went to sleep.

My stay in the silver city was brief; still attempting to stick to my self-imposed schedule I was soon on my way back to Mexico City. I took a taxi to John's apartment in Coyoacán once again. He was waiting to greet me with another of his celebrated pies. I spent the evening bringing him and El Lobo up to date with my adventures.

I had one free day in which to wander in the vast capital city. As always, the humidity, altitude and pollution prevented me from going very far. I walked around the elegant neighbouring suburb of San Angel, filled with beautiful villas and flowery bowers.

I took my hosts out to dinner in Coyoacán to thank them for their many acts of kindness. It was certainly the most upmarket restaurant I had eaten in so far and a pleasant contrast to Marco Pollo and other cantinas on my travels.

John and El Lobo told me more stories about Coyoacán, which means place of the coyote. Cortes set up his headquarters here in 1521 to plan his assault on the city of Tenochtitlan. The house he built for his mistress and interpreter, La Malinche, still stands today.

'Have you visited Trotsky's house?' they asked. 'It's now a museum and his ashes are buried there in an urn carved with a hammer and sickle.'

It only remained for me to thank my hosts for the last time before leaving on the final trip out to the Pacific cost.

21
Puerto Vallarta - Ending on a High C

I was standing on a terrace fringed with oleander and hibiscus: a small kidney shaped pool glittered in the midday sun as I waited for a woman called Dorrie.

She was an expatriate American who owned this small apartment building and I was a displaced, wandering Brit who had convinced her that I could afford to buy one of the units. I had not quite convinced myself but I was working on that.

The apartments were named after signs of the zodiac; Dorrie lived in Virgo. My sign, Libra, was unfortunately not available, but Leo and Pisces were for sale.

I sat by the pool gazing out over the red tiled roofs towards the distant Pacific. On my left I could see the peninsula covered in impenetrable jungle. On the far right the towers of the high rise hotels gleamed enticingly. An impossibly white cruise ship was anchored straight ahead in the Bahia de las Banderas, the biggest, bluest bay in the world; in fact it is the second largest.

The lovely, light-hearted town of Puerto Vallarta was made famous by Elizabeth Taylor and Richard Burton who put the place on the map while filming *Night of the Iguana*. Now it is a favourite bolt hole for North Americans seeking escapist vacations. None of this should deter anyone from beating a path there; the scenery and the general ambience were wonderful and to a traveller from the grey and chilly north, albeit one with an over-active imagination, even the little galleon bobbing off the town beach became my own personal ship ready for adventure and exploration. It was unimportant that it took tourists on tequila cocktail cruises.

I felt almost guilty that Puerto Vallarta had replaced San Miguel in my affections. Although I knew nobody in the town I felt completely at home from the moment I tottered off the bus after one more overnight coach trip and checked into the Pension Cartagena, another seedy backpacker venue, but the price was right. I was contemplating staying here without a qualm. When I discovered that flamenco classes were on offer and that Dorrie had an apartment for sale I knew I might never leave.

When Dorrie arrived, breathless from her aromatherapy massage, she turned out to be a widowed business woman who had used her savings to build the apartment block which provided her with a comfortable existence. She showed me around her own unit with its wonderful views over the bay, its exuberant Mexican tiling and locally made furniture.

'Don't forget the closets!' she exclaimed. 'I insisted on plenty of closet space.' I duly admired everything and said how much I would like to live there.

Mortgages were then unknown in Mexico and ownership would have involved changing sterling to dollars and then into pesos, as well as a brush with the complexities of Mexican law.

It was just a pipe dream brought on by the heat and the lush scenery. Still, if Dorrie had placed a contract in my hands I would have signed. I was saved by the fact that I did not have the money to hand for the deposit. I regret it to this day.

After making empty promises to Dorrie I dawdled back down the hill into the town. Mexican lunch smells wafted up to meet me, full of refried beans, chicken and charcoal fires. The iron crown atop the cathedral rose gracefully over the low-rise housing and the stray dogs did not bother to raise their heads from the gutters where they were taking a siesta.

I sat under a shady umbrella licking tamarind flavoured ice-cream. This is lotus eating country. Once you have sat on a terrace overlooking the Pacific watching an orange and carmine sunset sinking into the violet waters of the Bay of Flags, you forget that home is thousands of miles away together with your possessions, your books, your relatives and your problems. Here, you need only your dreams and a warm, tropical breeze on your face.

Puerto Vallarta was full of people chasing their dreams; the German who ran a scuba diving business, the English couple running the bookshop and the Americans who had come to retire in what had been dubbed gringo gulch. I met a few of them in various cafés. When I told them that my hotel cost only thirty per night they cried out in astonishment,

'Wow! Thirty dollars per night; that's really cheap!' I hadn't the heart to tell them that I meant thirty pesos.

Unwilling to give up the idea of living in a tropical haven, I continued searching for a small house that I could afford. A local Mexican-American estate agent or realtor showed me a place that was definitely not in gringo gulch but in a real street where real Mexicans lived. The house was pleasant enough but warning bells sounded when I saw that the previous owner had left all the furniture, which was riddled with termite holes.

While I was in Puerto Vallarta's small bus station I met an American family who were making a pilgrimage to a place called San Patrizio, named for a group of Irishmen, exiled by the British, who had fought with the Mexicans during their War of Independence. The Americans were of Irish origin and they were going to attend a fiesta that was always held on St Patrick's Day. They departed on their coach sporting shamrocks and waving Mexican flags. I remembered that it was March 16th and in ten days time I would be back in England.

I took a bus a few miles down the coast to Rincon de los Guayabitos which was simply a long and beautiful beach with small holiday apartments set among trees. There was a small village area equipped with shops and restaurants and a laundromat or two. The beach was almost empty with only a few sun-seekers, mainly elderly, North Americans and a handful of Mexican families.

It was a family resort which was probably packed later in the year - another good spot to spend the winter months. An elderly man was barbecuing fish on the beach and I bought one for a few pesos eating it on the sand with a slice of watermelon for dessert.

I was intrigued to learn that the billionaire entrepreneur James Goldsmith had a huge estate nearby. It was impossible to get near the place so I passed the time as I waited for the bus back to town by imaging how I would live if I was Jemima Khan, Goldsmith's daughter. I doubted that renting a palapa in Yelapa would be an option.

I was looking forward to the trip to Yelapa: the gringo cruise, as I had dubbed it, was a leisurely affair. On board we were given fruit as a late breakfast and we watched another shining white Norwegian cruise ship drop anchor in the bay. Nearby, a replica of one of the caravelles used by Columbus rode at anchor, bobbing absurdly on the waves like a beribboned cork, with its sails neatly furled ready for the next tequila excursion.

Only someone like Columbus, part visionary, part opportunist, part adventurer would have attempted to cross the Atlantic in something like that. Today the visionaries and adventurers in Puerto Vallarta go deep sea fishing.

'It's an inward journey today, man,' I heard one of them say to a passing backpacker.

As we crossed the bay various Canadians, retired and well-heeled, explained that they had come south for the sun, part of the retreat of the "snow birds" who come down to Mexico in droves from the frozen north.

'I can bear it until Christmas time,' said the man ahead of me in the juice queue, 'then I have to get out of Alberta.' His wife looked as if she would have preferred to stay at home. She scratched a mosquito bite and stared disconsolately out at the blinding azure water.

I had been told about Yelapa a few says earlier as I was walking on the ominously named Playa de Los Muertos (Beach of the Dead) in Puerto Vallarta.

'You can get a boat from the jetty,' I was advised. 'That's the only way to get there.' The lure of a desert island was a powerful one. Never mind that that it wasn't quite an island and not exactly deserted. Yelapa was a jewel of a place lying at the end of a peninsula covered in dense jungle. The only access was by a small boat across the Bay of Flags where you could expect to hit the beach as if on an SAS assault course. The boatmen hurled your luggage after you as you leapt into the surf.

'There is no electricity and the community is a small one,' my informant continued. 'You can rent a palapa, a thatched roof cabin, for a few dollars. There is nothing to do except enjoy the peace and the stunning views.' I decided to make a preliminary inspection by taking a morning cruise to this special place.

On Yelapa I sat on the beach drying my T-shirt while the mules waded across the river behind me. I thought about the trip over on the following day in Jose's water taxi. The pueblo end of the beach was the peaceful end with fewer, cheaper cafés and no vendors. The pie lady did not bother to bring her wares out to my rock and the boy with the iguana was off duty that day.

The other end of the beach had up market cabins for rent provided with their own electricity generator. The rest of the island made do with candles and oil lamps. Poverty and romantic notions propelled me into the small pueblo where I arranged to rent a fairly run down palapa for a modest sum.

There was a shower (tepid) and a small gas ring in the cabin, a few candles, a bed, a table and a chair. The palapa was open to the elements on three sides, although I was amused to see that Juan, my landlord, had put a padlock on the front door.

The next morning I dragged my bag to the jetty and embarked on the exhilarating ride across the bay in a small motor boat. We were soaked with spray as the little vessel bounded along. A school of dolphins leapt joyfully around us and the water shone deep violet blue in the brilliant sun. I felt as if I was in an anteroom of paradise. We stopped at one or two isolated villages on the peninsula before anchoring offshore in Yelapa's bay.

I bravely jumped into the water and my bag followed me getting only slightly soaked in the process. My palapa on Yelapa was hidden in the forest that covers most of the settlement. I had no visible neighbours although Juan had built himself a brick house on the proceeds of his rentals. The traditional Mayan huts were far more attractive and less likely to collapse in a hurricane.

There is a strict ritual for building a palapa among the Mayan people. The poles for the palapa or Na must be cut during a full moon to ensure maximum power. The poles are taken from all the native trees and various woods are allocated for specific parts of the house. Each piece of wood has a different name and a special function.

Women and children are recruited to dig holes in the sand for the insertion of the poles. An offering must be made in the form of a local spirit or anything that comes to hand, ranging from vodka to coca cola. Then the main roof or mother beam must be erected and nourished with a drink. Then the thatch must be made and many decisions taken about the best kind of materials. The poles and sticks of the house are held together by vines from the jungle. During a hurricane the wind will blow through the Na but will not destroy it. In Mexico things are still close to the earth despite the inroads of modern life.

I soon realized that going out at night would be hazardous. I had remembered to bring a torch but when the warm tropical night descended the blackness was total. I couldn't face picking my way over rocks and streams and thickets where snakes and other tropical beasties lived. Within an hour of my arrival I had discovered a brown recluse spider living in a corner of the palapa. These dangerous creatures liked to be left undisturbed and I certainly intended to do that. I read somewhere that they didn't move around much. I devoutly hoped so as I lay awake at night listening to the incredible noises from the jungle nearby, all perfectly natural, but terrifying to a city bred female.

I rose with the dawn and went to bed soon after nightfall when I could no longer read by torchlight. I explored Yelapa by daylight and sunned myself on the beach where I met a wonderful collection of oddball characters.

Although this little corner of Mexico has slipped off the tourist agenda to a large extent, it was very different in the 1960s. During the hippy era many celebrities spent time here, including the Beatles and the Rolling Stones.

Now, a few cafés remained and a man who took visitors into the interior on mules. In the pueblo there was a general store, a telephone booth, a small church and an even smaller school. A sprinkling of Americans lived in the interior, enjoying the alternative lifestyle but few stayed all year, especially during the hurricane season.

The oddballs also tended to be American; there was the young woman with no qualifications who didn't like work and who intended to sit on a tropical beach for as long as possible. I had a feeling that Josie would not achieve much in her life.

"El que no tranza no avanza," as they say in these parts, no guts, no glory.

A more entrepreneurial American woman sold bead jewellery made by the Huichol Indians in the north. She was one of the few outsiders permitted to enter their villages.

There was a woman called Tosca whose mother had been an opera singer. She lived on the island with several large dogs, entertaining visitors. She considered herself to be part of the scenery but she too left when the hurricanes started,

A number of writers and artists lived in the interior but I wondered how much work I would do if I lived on a tropical island. Although I wrote up my travel journal religiously I certainly did not find it easy to adopt the work ethic in Yelapa. Whenever I went to the general store I found the staff snoring quietly in the shade so the problem was obviously a universal one.

On the way back from the store I bought a corn cob on a stick and ate it in front of a hungry, tethered mule that almost exploded with lust for my treat. He ate the leftovers, including the stick.

That evening I had intended eating at Gloria's café which promised supper and live music, but when I left the palapa at around eight pm I walked into that unnerving tropical blackness. There were no lights in Juan's house and his dogs were barking. Afraid that they might be loose, I gave up and went to bed early, chiding myself for my wimpish behaviour.

Next morning the shower was so temperamental that I resorted to heating pans of water for my wash and café con leche. Rosita Forbes wrote about finding guests in her tropical shower in Brazil…

A regiment of horned beetles, moths the size of birds and frogs with suction pads for feet. It was disconcerting to see them hanging inverted, their padded feet adhering to wall or ceiling. The nicest visitor was a toad the size of a saucepan. He sat on the floor and ate the beetles. When I picked him up he talked hoarsely like an old man who has taken snuff.

Later I set out for the waterfall I had heard so much about. When I passed Juan's house he came out to tell me that I had not been locking the front door of my palapa properly. The idea that anyone would want to steal anything from my seedy lodging was absurd. I told him about my problems with the dogs and he laughed, saying that they wouldn't bite me. At the same time he threw a stick at one of the smaller beasts that was trying to chew my bare leg.

I reached the waterfall after a half hour walk. It was quite beautiful and I ate breakfast alone in the little café overlooking the gushing stream. The proprietor came to sit with me and talked about the old days when Yelapa was a celebrity hangout. He said that many writers had visited.

Back in the village I spent a couple of hours washing clothes and cleaning up my tropical hovel. This Robinson Crusoe business can be quite wearing. I can understand how relieved Rob must have been to find Man Friday. I finally settled down to write at midday.

That evening I smartened myself up as much as possible and headed for the small yacht club where everyone gathered on Saturday night, according to Tosca. Unable to face another dark, early bedtime, I braved the assembled Yankee hordes – big mistake. I was the only unaccompanied female and I felt very conspicuous until I was invited to share a table with a friendly Mexican family. I ate an enormous meal of grilled fish, rice and vegetables and I was persuaded to try the local fire water, a tequila based drink called Raicilla. I reached the palapa at ten pm, a very late night in these parts, and found I was unable to sleep after drinking coffee late at night.

Juan came around next morning to bring me clean sheets and a copy of the Yelapa newspaper dated 1988! It was full of news about famous visitors; Paul McCartney, The Grateful Dead, John Huston and a woman called Xaviera Hollander who had written a book called *The Happy Hooker*.

I read more about the local wildlife than I wanted to know, remembering the current inhabitants of the palapa. In true dromomaniac fashion I daydreamed about places I had yet to see. Rosita Forbes' description of up country Brazil stayed in my mind. It was another paradise.

Brazil seemed to me to be like the Book of Genesis. In the beginning there was forest. On succeeding days gamblers who dreamed in millions said,"
Let there be cocoa, rubber, coffee, cattle." The red earth responded with a prodigality that shook the scheme of creation.

Flamboyant trees spread their orange-flowered umbrellas over the gate. Bamboos were so ridiculously like ostrich feathers that I had a vision of gigantic green birds with their heads buried in the sand, so that their tails were tilted skywards.
Bougainvillaea poured over the fence and clung to the veranda where right of way was disputed by a creeper with vast golden bells. The oleanders were prim white stars, and cactuses, insensitive as the fingers of fate, stood beside a fountain. The borders were heaped with flowers, their colours dimmed by the dusk as patches in an old quilt. Glow worms burned on the grass and toads were discussing something momentous under a riotous crimson plant that Brazilians call "just foliage."

As I watched the sunset from the harbour wall I could not believe that I would be back in England in eleven days' time. This thought was so disconcerting that I managed to drop my notes into the sea.

By the end of my stay I had eaten in all the half-dozen cafés, ridden a mule into the interior, watched a dance class on the beach (I was too lazy to join in), eaten a selection of the pie lady's wares – the pineapple version was fabulous – and posed with the baby iguana owned by a local boy. Reluctantly, I prepared to return to Puerto Vallarta and the next leg of my journey to Guadalajara, from where I would fly to California, and then home

22
California-Home-The Journey Is Its Own Reward

From Puerto Vallarta I took a bus to Guadalajara, Mexico's second city, remembered from my earlier visit a lifetime ago. I stayed overnight and then flew to San Francisco. I wiped away a tear as the plane took off. I loved certain European cities like Venice and Prague but Mexico was definitely my favourite country.

I had not been in San Francisco for many years, but airports do not usually sear themselves into one's psyche. Nothing was familiar and everything was familiar, because airports are cloned all over the world. I took a taxi to my friends' house about forty minutes from the city. My surroundings, including the house, seemed very blonde and fresh and Californian. I was given a short tour of the neighbourhood – walking was seen as an eccentric hobby in these parts – before joining in my friend's birthday celebrations.

Next morning I took the local train into the city where I had spent several years of my life and where my son had been born. Two local lads in my carriage were desperately trying to pick up two visiting French girls but their efforts were getting a decidedly supercilious Gallic brush off.

I was in time to watch the St Patrick's Day parade down Market Street. It had all the features I remembered including the anti-British element. Onlookers cheered as the Union Jack was trailed in the dust. They would go crazy if anyone treated their flag in the same way.

Following the familiar tourist route I took a cable car ride down to Fisherman's Wharf and wandered through

Chinatown, revisiting familiar spots. The crowds and the traffic were greater than before. Eventually I took a bus out to our former neighbourhood for old time's sake.

We are often told that we should not go back; should not try to revisit the past. The attempt can result in overwhelming and unhinging nostalgia. The small apartment block where we lived in the Richmond district was on a street painted in blinding white and sugar candy colours gleaming in the bright sunlight. I recalled it as being more muted but perhaps I was pre-occupied in those days.

The area was no longer predominantly Russian as it was in our day; Japanese and Korean influences were very marked. At the end of the street I took photographs of the small park where my son had played, still remarkably the same.

The San Andreas Fault line ran almost parallel with the street and the underlying tension of living in an earthquake zone and "waiting for the big one" was mirrored by the tensions in my failing marriage, a kind of macabre slow waltz on the fault line.

The fact that the drama was played out against the backdrop of the Golden State rather than the grey streets of London made little difference. The occasional earth tremors reverberated with the bumps in the relationship. Like those Victorian women I should just have kept moving.

At least we were spared the Santa Ana wind that blew in Southern California - the wind that made meek housewives finger the blade of a carving knife and stare at their husband's neck – according to the crime writer Raymond Chandler.

Clement Street, our local shopping venue, had become much busier and more oriental and somehow larger than I remembered. I spotted one remaining Russian café where we used to buy piroshkis- a sort of fried bun filled with mincemeat, much better than it sounds.

The local Walgreen's store had been spruced up. I went inside to buy a bar of almond roca, still in its candy pink wrapper and redolent of old times; delicious teeth-rotting stuff, comfort food after marital rows. So many memories are of food; like Proust's madeleines they immediately conjure up the past.

Very little remained of those days except in my head, of course. The Grateful Dead playing at the local ballroom, hippydom installed in the Haight-Ashbury district and the Vietnam War in full swing. I recalled the bed we bought on Clement Street, its four posts topped with pineapple finials. It was shipped back to the UK at vast expense and disappeared in one of our many moves.

Golden Gate Park in all its splendour was nearby and a favourite place for pushing my son in his buggy. This lovely spot was created on sand dunes by a Scotsman in the nineteenth century. The Shakespeare garden was planted with all the herbs and flowers mentioned in the bard's plays. I met friends in the Japanese teahouse while my son greeted the local police horse. Magnolia trees bloomed in January and groups of hippies smoked joints furtively among the bushes. Nostalgia was threatening to cripple me so I boarded a bus back to the centre of the city.

My friends insisted on showing me around a vast shopping mall in Palo Alto. Americans find it hard to believe that we have anything similar. I tried to explain about Bluewater but they were not convinced.

In the early evening I said my goodbyes and took the shuttle to Los Angeles. My son arrived to have dinner with me on my last evening on American soil and we reminisced about our travels before saying goodbye.

Next morning I was offered a breakfast of pancakes, sausages, toast and trimmings that would have fed a family of six in most parts of the world.

I nibbled at the edges reflecting that I had only nibbled at the world on my travels. I had a way to go to catch up with my Victorian heroines, but they had spent years on the move. Perhaps I had done nothing more than pass the time pleasantly. The Italians coined a word for this, "asolare" based on the town of Asolo near Venice that was such a wonderful place in which to do very little. Freya Stark lived in Asolo and would have been familiar with this activity, but her travels were the real thing.

The flight home was ghastly: I had been allotted the last seat at the rear of the economy section on a crowded American Airlines plane. The amount of leg room was pitiful even for a person not much over five feet in height. The stewardesses were unfriendly and unwilling to attend to anyone. This airline had a distinctly feminist attitude to the job. Fine - but a smile now and then wouldn't hurt.

I glimpsed the occasional iceberg as we flew over the Pole and I chatted with a pleasant, English ex-pat now living in a small town in Texas. When I said that would be my idea of hell, he had the grace to laugh.

Already I could feel the bad attack of jet lag that always afflicts me on returning long haul flights fogging my brain and sapping my energy. This time I suffered a strange symptom that caused my face to become puffy and stiff. I fell into an uneasy doze, my mind buzzing with the events of the past year. A procession of those eccentric and lovable lady travellers paraded through my consciousness. By this time they were like sisters to me.

I thought drowsily of Kate Marsden and her plum puddings, May Sheldon with her white sequin gowns to impress the natives, Henriette d'Angeville climbing Mont Blanc for fun in a long skirt, corsets and a feathered bonnet, sustained by sponge cake and champagne and Isabelle Eberhardt careering madly around the desert on horseback.

My escapades seemed so tame in comparison, but I was with them in spirit.

Why did we do it? Why couldn't we just stay at home in the bosom of our families if we had them - or with our friends? I could hear those Mexican matrons, 'Pobrecita!' Henriette spelled it out-
The soul has needs as does the body, peculiar to each individual; and a desire to subordinate these needs to the general rule is as unreasonable as an attempt to bring up the weak on precepts laid down for the strong or vice versa ...In short, each of us must arrange his life according to his moral or intellectual inclinations. And so it is just as ridiculous to ask someone who is fond of travel, "why are you setting out?" as it is to say, "why are you staying at home?" to someone who loves seclusion.

I staggered off the plane at Heathrow in the early evening feeling distinctly peculiar. I joined an interminable queue for what I thought was passport control. I was the only white person in the line and the others were giving me curious looks. A passing airport official stopped and peered at my passport. She was a motherly Asian lady who gave a yelp and exclaimed;

'Oh God! You shouldn't be on this queue, they're all foreigners!" She propelled me firmly along to the correct line. 'Feeling a bit under the weather, are we?'

I boarded an airport bus to Euston but I have no memory of that journey other than the feeling that my face was twice its normal size. I wondered if I was developing the early signs of elephantiasis.

At Euston station in the rush hour the wait for taxis was a long one. As we seeped slowly into the virtually gridlocked traffic I began to shiver violently. It was almost April but it felt like November. I remembered Margaret Fountaine's reaction whenever she arrived back on these sunless shores.

Browning must have been suffering from loss of memory when he wrote "Oh! To be in England now that April's there!" I feel a longing to be away in some land of sunshine and hot rain.

I have the same reaction when I return by sea; the sight of the white cliffs of Dover always fills me with profound depression. This must be the sign of a true dromomaniac. I recalled the description of poor Margaret Fountaine given by an acquaintance- "Something of a loner with few friends and an uncontrolled wanderlust."

The taxi driver was looking at me in his mirror. His cheery whistling had given way to a worried frown.

'Feeling all right, love?' My lips seemed to be made of rubber.

'Yeth,' I mumbled, adding by way of explanation, 'I've been abroad.' The driver nodded understandingly.

'Been anywhere nice?' For a moment my mind went blank; where had I been during this eventful year? Then I remembered something.

'I was in Georgia,' I mumbled again.

'That's nice," he smiled, beginning to hum 'Georgia on my mind.'

'No, no...not that Georgia, I mean the one in the Caucasus, the former Russian Republic.' The driver looked worried again as he caught a glimpse of my pallid, puffy appearance.

'You should have gone to Tenerife, love. My missus wouldn't go anywhere else.'

When I finally collapsed on my mother's doorstep in North West London, she opened the door and appeared not to have noticed my long absence.

'Oh, it's you! I was just off to play bingo.'

End

Bibliography

1. Nine Pounds of Luggage-Maud Parrish (1939)
2. A Lady's Life in the Rocky Mountains - Isabella Bird Bishop (1873)
3. Unprotected Females in Norway - Emily Lowe (1854)
4. A Lady's Walks in the South of France - Mary Eyre (1863)
5. A Motor Flight through France - Edith Wharton (1908)
6. The Story of My Life - George Sand (1854)
7. Gypsy in the Sun - Rosita Forbes (1944)
8. By Desert Ways to Baghdad - Louise Jebb (1908)
9. Ten Days in Spain - Kate Field (1875)
10. Up the Country - Emily Eden (1866)
11. Lispings from Low Latitudes - Lady Dufferin (1863)
12. The Journals of Fanny Parkes (1850)
13. The Nomad - Isabelle Eberhardt (1987)
14. A Lady's Voyage around the World - Ida Pfeiffer (1852)
15. My Ascent of Mont Blanc - Henriette d'Angeville (1987)
16. A Sportswoman in India - Isabel Savory (1900)
17. Tight Corners of my Adventurous Life - Mrs Alec Tweedie (1933)
18. Life in Mexico - Mme. Calderon de la Barca (1843)
19. Sister of the Road: The Autobiography of Boxcar Bertha - Dr.Ben Reitman (2002)
20. The Turkish Embassy Letters - Lady Mary Wortley Montague (1837)
21. Love Among the Butterflies - Margaret Fountaine (1980)
22. Travels in West Africa - Mary Kingsley (1897)
23. On Sledge and Horseback to Outcast Siberian Lepers - Kate Marsden (1892)
24. A Thousand Miles up the Nile - Amelia Edwards (1878)
25. My Journey to Lhasa - Alexandra David-Néel (1927)

Made in the USA
Columbia, SC
20 June 2018